Beyond the
Window

Inside Your Heart

*Kim,
May you experience
the God who lives
Inside Your Heart!
Blessings,
Rachel*

RACHEL JOLLY WEST

Copyright © 2023 Rachel Jolly West.

All rights reserved. No part of this book may be used or reproduced by any means, graphic, electronic, or mechanical, including photocopying, recording, taping or by any information storage retrieval system without the written permission of the author except in the case of brief quotations embodied in critical articles and reviews.

This book is a work of non-fiction. Unless otherwise noted, the author and the publisher make no explicit guarantees as to the accuracy of the information contained in this book and in some cases, names of people and places have been altered to protect their privacy.

WestBow Press books may be ordered through booksellers or by contacting:

WestBow Press
A Division of Thomas Nelson & Zondervan
1663 Liberty Drive
Bloomington, IN 47403
www.westbowpress.com
844-714-3454

Because of the dynamic nature of the Internet, any web addresses or links contained in this book may have changed since publication and may no longer be valid. The views expressed in this work are solely those of the author and do not necessarily reflect the views of the publisher, and the publisher hereby disclaims any responsibility for them.

Any people depicted in stock imagery provided by Getty Images are models, and such images are being used for illustrative purposes only. Certain stock imagery © Getty Images.

Interior Image Credit: Rachel Jolly West, Hope Bain

ISBN: 978-1-6642-8728-0 (sc)
ISBN: 978-1-6642-8730-3 (hc)
ISBN: 978-1-6642-8729-7 (e)

Library of Congress Control Number: 2022923542

Print information available on the last page.

WestBow Press rev. date: 01/18/2023

Scripture quotations marked AMP are taken from the Amplified® Bible, Copyright © 1954, 1958, 1962, 1964, 1965, 1987 by The Lockman Foundation. Used by permission.

Scripture quotations marked ESV are from the ESV Bible® (The Holy Bible, English Standard Version®), copyright © 2001 by Crossway Bibles, a publishing ministry of Good News Publishers. Used by permission. All rights reserved.

Scripture quotations marked NKJV are taken from the New King James Version. Copyright © 1982 by Thomas Nelson, Inc. Used by permission. All rights reserved.

Scripture quotations marked NIV are taken from the Holy Bible, New International Version®, NIV®. Copyright © 1973, 1978, 1984 by Biblica, Inc.™ Used by permission of Zondervan. All rights reserved worldwide.

Scripture quotations marked NLT are taken from the Holy Bible, New Living Translation, copyright © 1996, 2004, 2007 by Tyndale House Foundation. Used by permission of Tyndale House Publishers, Inc., Carol Stream, Illinois 60188. All rights reserved.

Scripture quotations marked TLB are taken from The Living Bible copyright © 1971. Used by permission of Tyndale House Publishers, Inc., Carol Stream, Illinois 60188. All rights reserved.

Contents

Acknowledgments ix
Preface xi

100% Jesus 1
A One-of-a-Kind Compassionate God 3
A Time for Remembering Lightning Bugs (Fireflies) 8
Are You a Jack-O-Lantern? 12
Are You Focused? 14
Bloom! 17
Can We Pray When We Don't Feel Like It? 21
Discovering Ourselves 23
Don't Ever Give Up! 25
From the Other Side of the Lamp 28
Don't Steal Someone Else's Gift 31
Flying Untethered Can Be Dangerous! 33
Footprints of Discipleship 36
God's Everlasting Love 39
God's Best Nutrition Plan Ever! 43
Hangin' On By a Thread or Two Hands? 46
Hold On! 50
He Promised 52
How Do You Water Your Soul and Spirit? 55
How's Your Prayer Life? 59
I Wasn't Created to Bear It Alone 61
Is There Hope for These Dry Bones/Healing of the Nation 64

Jesus, the Bread of Life: How Far Would You Go To Get It?........68
The Joy of a Babe..71
The Roar of Spittin' Rain..75
Matters of the Heart...77
Oh No! Did I Miss that Opportunity?....................................80
Oh, What A Relief It Is!..83
OPEN All The Time!..86
Our God is More than a 3D Machine 89
Remain Constant in the Treatment Plan..............................92
Rise and Shine!..96
Rise from the Pool...99
That Simple Touch..102
The 5-Fold Ministry...105
The Babe That Melts our Hearts..107
The Beauty of His Holiness..109
The Deafening Silence of No Electrical Power!!..................112
The Deception of the Enemy...114
The First Step - A Risk or the Real Thing...........................116
Standing Alone can be Tough 119
The Gift that Keeps on Giving...122
The Golden Rule – It's About What We Give 124
The Protection of a Leaf..126
There Was Jesus..128
Trusting Without Borders 131
Letter to Santa..134
Upholstered by God..136
We Are In Transformation = WAIT!..................................138
What Happens to All of the Fallen Leaves?........................141
Who's Behind that Curtain?..144
Who Are You Standing Next To?......................................146

About The Author..149

Acknowledgments

To my Lord and Savior, Jesus Christ, all honor, glory, and majesty to You, now and forever. Thank you for every message in this book.

To my family – my personal and church families. Thank you for your support and encouragement!

To my prayer warriors who have prayed for me throughout this mission; who have supported this effort not only by prayer but also by their editing, consulting, and marketing recommendations and simply asking "How's the book going?" God, in His infinite Wisdom, knew that I would need each of you during the preparation and completion of His second book. I am beyond grateful for God connecting us for such as time as this and for such a Godly task as this.

> "You are God's opportunity in your day. He has waited for ages for a person just like you. If you refuse Him, then God loses His opportunity which He sought through you; and He will never have another, for there will never be another person on the earth just like you."
> (Cowman, L. B., "Springs in the Valley", (Michigan, Zondervan, 1939), 236).

God bless you all!

Preface

In July 2022, I took a step of faith, feeling God's nudging to begin His second book. I signed the WestBow Press's contract and thought of what steps to take. There were learnings with my authoring of the first book, *The View From My Window: A Walk With God*. One learning was to seek help! I contacted a good friend for her help and consultation with the book. She agreed with no hesitation.

A few days later I was reading a hand-out from my pastor/husband, Mike, which included prayers and scripture for 30 days of discernment for our church. As I read each day, I found that I had begun to substitute the word "book" in place of the word "church". These entries focused on discernment of where God was leading the church and steps we should take as a congregation. As I discovered along the way, those prayers became a focus for this book.

On the day I finished reading this document, I examined the pages and landed on "July 1". Here is the prayer and scripture for that day:

> Dear God, let your Spirit speak words of wisdom and guidance over my life today. You promised a Comforter who will be with me every step of the way to guide me and supply what I need. Be with me, Father. Help me make the right choices and choose the right opportunities. Making decisions can be confusing. Holy Spirit, fill me so I know the way God wants me to go. Help me determine which direction

will open the right doors and cause my church (book) to flourish. Amen.

"Therefore brethren, seek out from among you seven men of good reputation, full of the Holy Spirit and wisdom, whom we may appoint over this business." Acts 6:3 (NKJV)

The disciples were overwhelmed with the number of new disciples and the time they were spending away from the ministry of the Word of God. The widows and poor needed to be cared for, so the disciples asked for seven men to be responsible for this undertaking.

When I finished reading this scripture, I felt God telling me to make a list of "seven people of good reputation and full of the Holy Spirit." I made a list. The names came easily, and these persons are the prayer warriors in my life. God told me to have these people begin praying over this book. I immediately called each person and shared this experience with them. They agreed without hesitation to come alongside God and me in this venture.

Little did I know how much I would need these prayers, but God knew! There have been numerous interruptions to my work on His book – physical problems, ministry needs, family needs, etc. The enemy has been busy.

However, the prayers of these prayer warriors have been felt and heard! This is God's second book, and His book is going forth around the world. His request in the first book was that "These messages are for all believers around the world."

Thank you, God, for launching Your Word! May it fly high, *Beyond the Window: Inside Your Heart*

100% Jesus

> "You will seek me and find me when you seek me with all your heart."[1]

I recently signed up for an online Bible study entitled, "Get Out of Your Head". As the title of the study obviously implies, the focus was what we tend to think about most of the time. The second week's study, written by Jennie Allen, shared the following (emphasis mine).

> We have to figure out what it is that we love more than God. What is the thing we're chasing? What would happen if Jesus replaced the main goal in your life?[2]

In my brain, I felt stunned and had to let that sink in! Don't I already have Jesus as the main goal in my life – to work toward becoming more like Him? If Jesus is the *main* goal in my life, I should have Jesus in my thoughts, my actions, and my words 100 percent of the time. Right? Then the remaining goals would fall into place.

I must admit that Jesus is not always in my thoughts, actions, or words 100 percent of the time. I love thinking of ways to help others, but I also focus on myself and what I *think* I need. This coronavirus has brought my laziness to newer heights, especially when it comes

---

[1] Jeremiah 29:13 (NIV).
[2] Allen, Jennie, "Get Out of Your Head", accessed January 29, 2020, https://www.studygateway.com/.

to cleaning the house. I have spent more money than usual on new outfits because of my younger son's wedding activities. I have spent more money at the grocery store trying new recipes. I have continued my long-standing relationship with Amazon by purchasing books and household items we have needed. I have focused on these things and not necessarily on Jesus! Also, I have made plans without necessarily involving Jesus in the decision-making processes. Can anyone relate?

But the crux of the matter is this:

> *Probably, the thing you fixate on, is also the thing you worship. No matter what we lose in this life — opportunities, relationships, pleasures, jobs, money, prestige, reputations, friendships, possessions — none of it compares to Him The rest will work out however it works out. For good or for bad.*[3]
>
> *"What would happen if Jesus replaced the main goal in your life?"* [4]

Is it unrealistic to think of focusing on Jesus 100 percent of the time? I don't know, but I will work towards that 100 percent of Jesus. Why? Because He is the One to think about All the time! Everything else will work out.

Go hard for God. Go hard after Jesus!

---

[3] Allen, Jennie, "Get Out of Your Head", accessed January 29, 2020, https://www.studygateway.com/.

[4] Allen, Jennie, "Get Out of Your Head", accessed January 29, 2020, https://www.studygateway.com/.

A One-of-a-Kind Compassionate God

"I have loved you, my people, with an everlasting love."[5]

Do you ever wonder why God doesn't give up on us because of our disobedience? Can God really be this caring and compassionate? In the Old Testament, He is constantly rescuing the Israelites when they cry out to Him after their disobedience. In the New Testament, He went so far as to send His only Son to die for us, defeat sin and death, and redeem us! Still there is disobedience--even now in our generation--but He rescues us when we cry out!

While reading my Bible, I was captured by the farewell address of Joshua to the Israelites before he died and the warning he gave them (emphasis mine).

> "Soon I will die, going the way of everything on earth. Deep in your hearts you know that *every promise of the Lord your God has come true. Not a single one has failed*! But as surely as the Lord your God has given you the good things he promised, he will also bring disaster on you if you disobey him. He will completely destroy you from this good land he has given you. If you break the covenant of the Lord your God by worshiping and serving other gods, his anger

---

[5] Jeremiah 31:3 (NLT).

will burn against you, and you will quickly vanish from the good land he has given you."[6]

Fair warning, I think. This is how Judges 2 begins:

> "After that generation died, another generation grew up who did not acknowledge the LORD or remember the mighty things he had done for Israel. The Israelites did evil in the LORD's sight and served the images of Baal. They abandoned the LORD, the God of their ancestors, who had brought them out of Egypt. They went after other gods, worshiping the gods of the people around them. And they angered the LORD."[7]

Are we surprised at this? Does this sound familiar in our generation? But wait...what did God do? Yes, he became very angry with them, and He even fought against them. He let them be defeated by every enemy. Then He raised up a judge to rescue the Israelites.

> "Whenever the Lord raised up a judge over Israel, he was with that judge and rescued the people from their enemies throughout the judge's lifetime. For the Lord took pity on his people, who were burdened by oppression and suffering."[8]

After the Israelites' behavior and lack of obedience to the Lord, the Lord *still* took pity on his people. I call Him a **one-of-a-kind, compassionate God**. When His people cried out for help, the Lord rescued them by raising up a "rescuer".

I bring this to your attention because of our current situation with COVID-19 as well as our history of obedience and disobedience to God. I remember 9/11 and what an awful, horrendous happening

---

[6] Joshua 23:14-16 (NLT).
[7] Judges 2:10-12 (NLT).
[8] Judges 2:18 (NLT).

that was, in which so many people – almost 3,000 – were killed. The COVID-19 virus has already killed over 50,000 people in the United States alone in just a few months. What a time to reach out to our Lord and Savior!

After 9/11, there was a tremendous surge in church attendance, but it waned after about three months. What do you think will happen first when our country is slowly reopened after the virus? Will people seek God? Will they go to the beach? Will they go out to eat at their favorite restaurants? Will they greet their neighbors? Have we learned that God is giving us an opportunity to seek Him during this pandemic?

What will we do first and foremost? Will we repeat our "9/11" behavior and abandon God in a few months only to call on Him if/when the virus returns in the fall? God is ready to receive *all* of us whether we know Him or not. He is a compassionate God; He sent His only Son (the Lamb of God) to bring us into a new covenant with Him. *I call Him a one-of-a-kind, compassionate God.*

I wonder if we are telling/demonstrating God to the next generation – what He has done, what He is doing, and what He will do if we turn to Him and repent. Along with the preachers, it is now *our* responsibility to tell the next generation about God. Are we going to be like the generations after Joshua and disavow or abandon God, turning away from Him to worship an idol which we can see and touch? I pray not.

Consider God's track record (emphasis mine). *"Every promise of the Lord your God has come true. Not a single one has failed!"*[9] He is the same now.

Long ago the Lord said to Israel: "I have loved you, my people, with an everlasting love.

With unfailing love I have drawn you to myself."[10]

"I am the Lord, and I do not change."[11]

---

[9] Joshua 23:14 (NLT).
[10] Jeremiah 31:3 (NLT).
[11] Malachi 3:6 (NLT).

We have seen God's people repeat these patterns of behavior in the past and all through the years to the present.

What will we do first and foremost? I pray that we will continue (or begin) to worship God in the highest and most sincere way possible, filled with praises and prayer. *Join me as I call Him a one-of-a -kind, compassionate God!*

A Time for Remembering Lightning Bugs (Fireflies)

"Let your light shine before others, that they may see your good deeds and glorify your Father in heaven."[12]

When spring arrives, I am waiting expectantly for the first lightning bug to light up! To me, that has always signified the beginning of summer – being out of school, going on vacations, swimming in the lake, boating for hours, etc. Who did *not* get that pint or quart jar, poke holes in the lids, and fill it with lightning bugs (or fireflies as some people call them)? What memories!

I was watching these bugs from the porch the other night and realized that I really didn't know much about them, so God showed me! Here is a portion of what I found from this link that I was led to read:[13]

1. "They are beetles, not flies.
Fireflies are nocturnal members of *Lampyridae*, a family of insects within the beetle order Coleoptera (or winged beetles). They are officially beetles. And bonus fact: the family name,

---

[12] Matthew 5:16 (NIV).
[13] Breyer, Melissa, "11 Things You Didn't Know About Fireflies", updated January 10, 2021, https://www.treehugger.com/fireflies-things-you-didnt-know-about-lightning-bugs-4864255.

Lampyridae comes from the Greek *lampein,* meaning to *shine* just like a lamp."

➢ God has given us all the capability to shine like a lamp!

2. "They are alchemists, poetically speaking at least.
   While they don't turn base metals into gold, they do create light. When a chemical called luciferin inside their abdomen/tail combines with oxygen, calcium and adenosine triphosphate, a chemical reaction creates their spectacular light."

➢ Upon accepting Jesus Christ as our Lord and Savior, a reaction quickens the light of Christ within us, and we can demonstrate it outwardly through our behaviors and words.

3. "There are fireflies in the western United States; they just lack the "fire".
   California has perfect weather, palm trees, and stellar food. But alas, it doesn't have fireflies. California doesn't have fireflies that light up. Of the more than 2,000 species of fireflies, only some come equipped with the ability to glow; the ones that can glow do not generally live in the West."

➢ Those who do not know God simply cannot shine the light of Christ. The light of Christ comes from the east, and we must go to those toward the west who don't have the light and share it with them.

4. "They are light geniuses.
   Firefly light is incredibly efficient. The light produced by the firefly is the most efficient light ever made. Almost 100 percent of the energy in the chemical reaction is emitted as light; in comparison, an incandescent light bulb only emits

10 percent of its energy as light; the other 90 percent is lost as heat."

➢ Isn't it just like God to create the lightning beetle with the most efficient light ever made? He created it to use all its energy to shine its light each time it blinks. Are we doing that?

5. "They come in a rainbow of colors.
While they may not make up the whole spectrum of a rainbow, they do come in yellow, light red, green and orange."[14]

➢ These colors mean the following in God's language:

Yellow - Faith and Glory of God, Anointing, Joy, Spiritual Enlightenment
Red - Love of God, Blood of Lamb, Atonement, Salvation, Understanding
Green - Praise, Growth, Prosperity, New Beginning, Flourishing, Restoration,
Orange - Fire of God, Deliverance, Passionate Praise, Counsel

To summarize:

- Fireflies are beetles.
- They create a spectacular light.
- Not all fireflies are capable of creating light..
- The light is the most efficient ever
- The lights come in various colors.

Isn't that what God did in creating us?
He created us as human beings to connect with the family of *Lampyridae*, which means "shine". We are all capable of shining if we

---

[14] Breyer, Melissa, "11 Things You Didn't Know About Fireflies", updated January 10, 2021, https://www.treehugger.com/fireflies-things-you-didnt-know-about-lightning-bugs-4864465.

choose. We must make that choice knowing that when we accept Jesus, our light will be shining at 100 percent effectiveness for Him! No energy will be lost but all will be focused on Him. We will be equipped with the four colors which give us faith and anointing; understanding and salvation; growth and new beginnings; counsel and passionate praise.

Our God is an awesome God – Creator, Sustainer, Giver of Life and Light!

Are You a Jack-O-Lantern?

"In the same way, let your light shine before men, that they may see your good deeds and glorify your Father in heaven"[15]

When we were preparing for our weekly lesson with the pre-school children at Centenary, we decided to teach them about a Jack-O-Lantern. What a "Jesus" lesson it was!

When Mike began the lesson, he asked the children if they knew what a Jack-O-Lantern was. None of them knew, but they recognized the pumpkin and wanted to carve it for Halloween. Mike proceeded to explain to them the process for carving a "face" on the pumpkin.

He explained that the first thing to do was to clean the pumpkin by washing off the dirt and mud on the outside. Then he took a sharp knife and cut a hole in the top of the pumpkin. After that, the fun part was to clean out the inside - scoop out all the seeds and yucky stuff.

He drew a "face" on one side of the pumpkin. It was a "face" that included triangular shaped eyes and nose. The mouth was sort of curved with a few teeth included. We wanted a happy Jack-O-Lantern!

He proceeded very carefully to carve a face by cutting out the eyes, nose, and mouth.

Then he put a battery-operated candle inside the Jack o' Lantern.

---

[15] Matthew 5:16 (NIV).

When the candle was turned on and the room lights turned off, the light shone through the eyes, nose, and mouth.

By this time, the kids were amazed! They saw the washing of the pumpkin, scraping out of the insides, drawing/carving a face, and the turning on of the light inside the Jack-o-Lantern.

Now doesn't this sound like how Jesus changes us? This is a pretty good picture of what happens when we invite Jesus into our hearts.

When we proclaim Jesus Christ to be our Lord and Savior, He cleanses us of our sin from the outside of our life to the inside. He removes all the yucky thoughts and the seeds of doubt, hate, and selfishness that we have inside and replaces them with fruits of the spirit – "love, joy, peace, longsuffering, kindness, goodness, faithfulness, gentleness, and self-control".[16] He gives us reasons to smile and puts his light inside to shine for all the world to see.

What will your thoughts be when you see a Jack-O-Lantern next time? I hope you will think of Jesus. Think about how he came to take away the sins of the world and put his light in our hearts to shine for Him.

---

[16] Galatians 5:22-23 (NKJV).

Are You Focused?

"...and the boat was already a considerable distance from land, buffeted by the waves because the wind was against it."[17]

This scripture in Matthew 14:22-33 is a familiar one. The disciples were in a ship crossing the sea when the wind began to blow stronger and stronger. The boat was being tossed, and they became afraid. They saw a figure walking on the water, and Peter recognized it as Jesus. Jesus called for Peter to come to Him. Peter began walking on the water toward Jesus but became afraid and began to sink. The winds ceased blowing when Jesus and Peter came into the boat.

This is a very familiar story from the New Testament; a story that is shared for its teaching moments; a story that is easily applied in today's culture and society. As Mike was reading this scripture in preparation for his Sunday service message, certain words stood out to me:

Verse 24: "The ship was ...tossed with waves: for the wind was contrary." Sounds like one of our summer afternoon thunderstorms, but look at these meanings. "Tossed"[18] means to fling with a sudden motion, tilt suddenly, make uneasy. "Contrary"[19] means opposite,

---

[17] Matthew 14:24 (NIV).
[18] *Merriam-Webster Dictionary*, "Tossed", https://www.merriam-webster.com/dictionary/tossed.
[19] *Merriam-Webster Dictionary*, "Contrary", https://www.merriam-webster.com/dictionary/contrary.

non-conforming, against. The wind was providing a distraction for the disciples and a scary one at that! They were not thinking about Jesus right now; only how to survive! Where did that fear come from?

Peter had to "come down" from the inside of the boat, or from his comfort level, so he had to humble himself and "come down" before Jesus.

<u>Verse 30</u>: Peter demonstrated his rock-solid faith by confidently walking on the sea water while he kept his eyes on Jesus. But then there was a distraction – the wind became boisterous, and he became afraid. He took his eyes off Jesus, and he began to sink and cried out for help.

<u>Verse 31</u>: As soon as Peter cried "Help", Jesus immediately reached out to catch Peter. Jesus is always with us; always lending a hand; always encouraging us.

I thought about Adam and Eve. Eve was distracted and persuaded against God by Satan. She ate the lie that he told her, and Adam did the same. Their eyes were being turned away from God at that instant, and they began to sink into sin. They took their eyes off God and began to sink away from the Garden and away from God.

Haven't we all been through this ourselves? We have taken our eyes away from Jesus, and we all know those various reasons why. There are many lessons here, but let's believe first that we have the boldness and perseverance to get out of the boat - to "come down out of the boat" and bow at the feet of Jesus. That is a *big* step, but at the same time, we must keep our eyes focused on Jesus. There will be so many other distractions – weather, family, work, relationships, etc. because the enemy will not rest.

Sarah Young described this very well in *Jesus Calling: Turn Toward Me,* (2019):

> Just as a spinning ballerina must keep returning her eyes to a given point to maintain her balance, so you must keep returning your focus to Me (*Jesus*). Circumstances are in flux, and the world seems to

be whirling around you. The only way to keep your balance is to *fix your eyes on Me*, the One who never changes. If you gaze too long at your circumstances, you will become dizzy and confused. Look to Me, refreshing yourself in My Presence, and your steps will be steady and sure.[20]

Let us keep our eyes focused on Jesus.

---

[20] Sarah Young, *Jesus Calling*, (Tennessee, Thomas Nelson, 2011), 120.

Bloom!

> "...for when the way is rough, your patience has a chance to grow. So let it grow, and don't try to squirm out of your problems. For when your patience is finally in full bloom, then you will be ready for anything, strong in character, full and complete."[21]

Have you ever been at the point when your emotional and spiritual accounts went bankrupt? Empty? The big, fat zero? I did earlier this year, and it was an experience I have never had before. Let me summarize it for you.

I had been totally immersed spiritually, emotionally, and mentally with preparing for and coordinating registration for a women's faith-based conference for several months. I experienced God's move in my life like never before - through frequent opportunities for praying with friends through texts, emails, and in person; through God's healing from two broken bones in my right leg; and through opportunities given to me by God to speak prophetically to friends. After the conference, I felt lost, and I found myself wondering what I was supposed to do next.

Then my husband and I were both sick with a stomach virus, (hadn't been sick in fifteen years!), and I later took him to the Emergency Room for bladder issues. Yes, one right after the other!

At a post-conference meeting of the women's conference, I had

---
[21] James 1:3-4 (TLB).

a sinking feeling inside of me, like I had run out of energy, and everything was closing in around me. When we prayed to end the meeting, I thanked God for what he had done for Mom recently, and then my mind was a complete blank. A complete blank! I couldn't say anything! By the time I got home, I felt like my spiritual account was at "0", and I just had to get away. It wasn't so much a type of depression but an emptiness that I couldn't refill. I had never experienced feeling anything like that before.

After many days that included praying over this situation, I was asking God to show me something – ANYTHING – to give me some encouragement and direction. The next day, I read in my devotional book, *Commanding Your Morning* by Cindy Trimm, about seeds and how it takes a long time for them to sprout. Just because we don't see them doesn't mean they aren't there and growing. It takes patience. The author says, "We need to believe and speak as if it is coming today but persist in our faith even if it takes decades.[22]" What a reminder and an encouragement!

The next day I saw this on Facebook.

> "When you are in a dark place, you sometimes tend to think you've been buried.
> Perhaps you've been planted. **Bloom**"[23]

It was as if the light bulb was flipped on when I read this. My inner spirit rose like a flower reaching up to the sun (or the SON!). This is exactly what I needed to hear as a reminder that there is more than one way to look at our circumstances.

After reading the word "BLOOM", this is what God gave me.

---

[22] Cindy Trimm, *Commanding Your Morning Daily Devotional* (Florida, Charisma House, 2014), 90.
[23] BA FF JV, June 30, 2020, https://m.facebook.com/BAFFJV/?paipv=0&eav=AfbkaKv_s8NM28-NxLlKZMKN5z_fxDqKZI8NJsVgdvHEk0Q2mHIOgjjFOEUl2-lSi4s.

When God says, "**Bloom**," He is saying:

B̲e

L̲ed

O̲ut

O̲f

M̲isery (unhappiness, hardship, discomfort, grief, worry, trial, tribulation, calamity, misfortune)

Bloom means a flourishing, healthy condition; the time or period of greatest beauty, artistry, etc.; to flourish or thrive, to be in or achieve a state of healthful beauty and vigor.[24]

This is how God wants us to be. Not in a state of misery but a state of bloom in which we can thrive and flourish for Him! I thank and praise Him for refilling me! Praise God!

---

[24] *Collins Dictionary*, "Bloom", https://www.collinsdictionary.com/us/dictionary/english/bloom.

Can We Pray When We Don't Feel Like It?

"Pray continually."[25]

Who doesn't need to pray continually in this day and age? My prayers will vary greatly in length and content. Sometimes my focus is just not there, but then I will find myself praying throughout the day. Sometimes it is plain hard for me to pray. Either I don't feel like it; I don't know what to pray; or I don't have the words to put into a prayer. We all have these times, don't we?

As I read my devotional this morning, the author began with the question: "Is it hypocritical to pray when we don't feel like it?" Before she answered her question, she shared the following thoughts:

> "If the soul *perseveres* in a life of prayer, there will come a time when *these seasons of dryness will pass away and the soul will be led out,* as Daniel says, *"into a spacious place" (Psalm 18:19). Let nothing discourage you.*
>
> When we are listless about prayer, *it is the very time when we need most to pray. The only way we can overcome listlessness in anything is to put more of ourselves, not less, into the task.*

---

[25] 1 Thessalonians 5:17 (NIV).

When you cannot pray as you would, pray as you can."[26]

Finally, Cowman gave an answer to her question:

"To pray when you do not feel like praying is not hypocrisy - it is faithfulness to the greatest duty of life. Just *tell the Father* that you don't feel like it – ask Him to show you what is making you listless. *He will help us to overcome our moods* and give us courage to persevere in spite of them."

We need to be encouraged and to give encouragement to others. It is more important than ever to stand for/with God than to stand for worldly objects/persons.

May God bless each of you, and may God bless our country!

---

[26] Cowman, L. B., "Springs in the Valley", (Michigan, Zondervan, 1939), 177-178.

Discovering Ourselves

"Let all that I am wait quietly before
God, for my hope is in him."[27]

A college friend posted this on Face Book. It caught my eye and grabbed my attention when it reappeared as a "Memory". It was taken from a Christmas card she received, and it was written by Michael Podesta.

> *If, as Herod, we fill our lives with things, and again with things;*
>
> *if we consider ourselves so unimportant that we must fill every moment of our lives with action, when will we have the time to make the long, slow journey across the desert as did the magi?*
>
> *Or sit and watch the stars as did the shepherds?*
>
> *Or brood over the coming of the child as did Mary?*
>
> *For each one of us there is a desert to travel,*
> *a star to discover, and*
> *a Being within ourselves to bring to life.*[28]

---

[27] Psalm 62:5 (NLT).
[28] Michael Podesta, *"If, as Herod, we fill our lives with things, and again with things"*, March 10, 2021, https://m.facebook.com/podestagraphics/posts

I don't know about you, but I needed this thought-provoking reminder right now. I don't really consider myself unimportant, but I do desire to fill my life with "moments of action", always "doing something".

Right now is the time to take a look at that desert each of us is traveling through and just how we are traveling through it. *Right now* is the time to seek to discover a "star" (which may or may not be a star in the sky), but something we seek to follow with our whole hearts. *Right now* is the time to keep in tune with the Being that is alive inside us, this Being called the Holy Spirit. *Right now* is the time to reflect upon that first Christmas when God gave us His very best: His Son, Jesus!

Praying that this powerful reminder will invade your spirit with the Hope that Christmas brings. May it never fade but continue its light, which is the light of Jesus Christ.

Merry Christmas to All!

Don't Ever Give Up!

"Blessed is the one who perseveres under trial because, having stood the test, that person will receive the crown of life that the Lord has promised to those who love him."[29]

Recently, I saw a dragonfly. As I was standing outside a donut shop in town waiting for a friend, this dragonfly appeared and was hovering above me. Or at least I thought he was hovering. He appeared to stay in this one space as though he was trying to decide where to go, but the wind picked up and blew hard against him. He then seemed to force himself to go straight ahead into the wind. It was him against the wind!

Standing there watching him dart around in the cloud-filled, blue sky, I was mesmerized by his incredibly fast movements. First, he veered to the right; then suddenly he was turning sharply to the left. When the wind picked up, it appeared he became more determined to stand against the wind and face it "head on". Veering to the right or left. he seemed to be "teasing" the wind as though the wind might be thinking it could defeat him and knock him to the ground. Before I could blink, the dragonfly had returned to his spot near me. I am certain this entire adventure had gone on for three or four minutes when suddenly, the dragonfly flew off, and my friend arrived asking why I was looking into the sky so intensely!

---

[29] James 1:12 (NIV).

Later, when I had time to reflect on this adventure, I realized that as I had watched the feat of this dragonfly, I found myself thinking of the "head on" battles we often face when the enemy appears "out of the blue" and attempts to knock us off our intended course. Sometimes it is easier than others to keep pushing forward past him. Sometimes we MUST turn to the right or the left to catch our breath and get back on course in spite of his interference. The enemy can really push hard against us, can't he?

My spirit rejoiced when I saw the strategic maneuvers of this dragonfly. I wanted to cheer him on! He knew what he was doing, and he knew just how to get beyond this pesky wind and to stay on his determined path!

> "Dragonflies are expert fliers. They can fly straight up and down and hover like a helicopter. If they can't fly, they'll starve because they only eat prey they catch while flying. Nearly all of the dragonfly's head is eye, so they have incredible vision that encompasses almost every angle except right behind them."[30]

The dragonfly has several advantages: being an agile flier; ability to fly up/down or hover like a helicopter; being the fastest insect; having an eye that allows it to see every angle. Do you wish you had some of these features? Perhaps some of these advantages would come in mighty handy, especially when it comes to facing the enemy. It does sound compelling, but we already have someone who is mightier than all of the advantages within all creation!

We have our God, who can cover us from every angle; who can move faster than any insect; who can hover above and below and all around us, and who can see in all directions.

God is more powerful than any "wind" the enemy can throw at us. We don't really have to turn to the right or the left to dodge the

---

[30] Sarah Zielinski, "14 Fun Facts About Dragonflies", October 5, 2011, https://www.smithsonianmag.com/science-nature/14-fun-facts-about-dragonflies-96882693/

problems but can face each one straight on with the power of the Almighty God within us.

We worship a mighty and effective God who wants us to grow stronger as we face the "wind" of the enemy, and He will help us. He knows what we are capable of, and I think He wants us to have the determination of this dragonfly. Don't let some attacks of the enemy blow you in a different direction from where you are going! Fight back but do it *In Jesus' Name*!

There is no name more powerful than the name of Jesus!

From the Other Side of the Lamp

"Therefore...pray for each other so that you may be healed. The prayer of a righteous person is powerful and effective."[31]

She sat quietly in the waiting room, alone but not alone. She was praying to the God who hears all our prayers. She was praying for her relative who was about to receive that difficult news from her test results. Oh, how she was praying within herself, with her love flowing from her heart to the God who knows her heart inside and out. She was praying.

There was a table and lamp next to her. Others were sitting on the other side of this table and lamp. Their conversation penetrated her praying as she heard them reference "Clarksville". She was not going to "eavesdrop", but what did she do? She began praying for those individuals, the ones on the other side of the lamp.

We don't know what is happening in the lives of those around us; we don't know if they are suffering or rejoicing inside; we don't know what they are facing when they enter those doors where the answers await. But God knows! That is why we pray! Yes, the Word tells us we are called to pray for others -- even for those we may not know.

Scripture tells us:

---

[31] James 5:16 (NIV).

> "Your word is a lamp for my feet,
> a light on my path."[32]

A lamp on a table gives off light which shines away from the lamp in the direction dictated by the shape of the lamp shade. Since we have God's Word in us, we also share His light through our prayers as dictated and directed by Him to those He has placed around us. Even as we pray silently, those prayers are on a trajectory straight to God, and His loving comfort shines back on his children in need. Our whispers of 'Thank-You' can be felt with each external display or internal emotion of joy and rejoicing.

> "When Jesus spoke again to the people, he said, 'I am the light of the world. Whoever follows me will never walk in darkness, but will have the light of life.'"[33]

God's Word is that light which can brighten and illuminate our daily walk and travels. We must read, listen, share, and follow the Word by remembering to pray for our loved ones, our neighbors, and total strangers on the other side of the lamp.

---

[32] Psalm 119:105 (NIV).
[33] John 8:12 (NIV).

Don't Steal Someone Else's Gift

"A man's mind plans his way [as he journeys through Life], but the LORD directs his steps *and* establishes them."[34]

Some of us who are gifted as being "helpers" are usually ready to jump to the aid of others when there is a need – cooking a meal, providing transportation, making a grocery store run, etc. Who wouldn't do what is needed for a friend?

Sometimes when I am at "loose ends", I may jump at something to do because I'm not sure what God wants me to be doing at that time. If someone mentions a need that I hear about, I am ready to help. Even if I hear about it third hand, I'll jump in. Sounds good, right?

Of course, God wants us to love others, which includes helping to provide what they need. But what if God doesn't want you to be the one to help this person or that situation? What if God has chosen someone else for that purpose? If God hasn't indicated to me in some way that He needs me to intervene, I need to stay put – however hard that is for me!

I have a friend who has been serving some family members as God has directed her, but today, the Holy Spirit told her to let this most recent need for assistance go to someone else. Her body and mind had been going non-stop for quite a while. She was able to rest

---
[34] Proverbs 16:9 (AMP)

for two days. She told me later that the Holy Spirit let her know that someone else was taking care of the situation – not her. This was her time to be still, rest, and re-energize.

What she said to me was this: "The Holy Spirit makes me strong and focused to do His will - what He calls me to do - and He gives me the directives, strength, and gifts to use when He calls me."

Listen to the Holy Spirit. Don't try to do what God hasn't called you to do. When He needs you, He will let you know and make you strong to do what He calls you to do.

If we intervene when God hasn't directed it, we could be "stealing" someone else's gift and their joy.

Flying Untethered Can Be Dangerous!

"Then we will no longer be immature like children. We won't be tossed and blown about by every wind of new teaching. We will not be influenced when people try to trick us with lies so clever, they sound like the truth."[35]

Recently I purchased a red mylar balloon to use at a book signing for the purpose of attracting the attention of customers to my specific location in the restaurant. After the event, I brought the balloon home and left it unleashed in the dining/kitchen area. I enjoyed seeing it every day as it floated near the ceiling untethered.

This morning I went grocery shopping, and when I returned, the balloon was not in the same area. Where was it? I walked through my office and into the family room, and I spotted it in there, near the bay window! I guess it was looking at the "view from my window"! HA! Well, I dutifully brought it back to the dining/kitchen area and left it there, so it could hang around.

Because the weather was so gorgeous today, I ate lunch outside on the patio where I began thinking about that balloon. It had been able to float away because it was not anchored or tied down to a heavier object. The currents from the HVAC system had likely moved it from one room to the next. As I finished my lunch, I wished I could have watched a video recording of all that movement!

---

[35] Ephesians 4:14 (NLT).

God shared with me how we humans are so easily tossed, thrown, and/or dragged here and there, just as the balloon, if we are not anchored down. And not just anchored down to any heavy object but anchored down to the right source – Christ!

An anchor is "someone or something that gives support when needed."[36]

We need an anchor in our lives to keep us grounded; to keep us tied to a reliable source who will move the anchor to keep us on *His* course; to keep us focused on what He wants/needs us to do for Him. If we are not anchored, we will be drawn off the course to a dark and dangerous path.

Who do you think will be pulling us away from where God wants us to be? Yep! The enemy will be glad to pull our rope and steer us in some crazy kind of direction that will lead us down the wrong path and into the stormy seas.

> "But let him ask in faith, with no doubting, for he who doubts is like a wave of the sea driven and tossed by the wind. For let not that man suppose that he will receive anything from the Lord; *he is* a double-minded man, unstable in all his ways."[37]

Let us not float around wherever the currents and teachings are towing us. Let us be intentional about who teaches us and what we read. We must take a stand for the One who created us; died for us; and gave us eternal life. The One who has plans for our lives will lead us if we will anchor ourselves to Him and surrender to Him. Our anchor ropes are faith, trust, hope, and love. We need to stay tethered to our Source with these ropes.

Don't fly out of control and lose your way. Anchor yourself to the One who will never budge from you. He will always be steady and strong for you. And He loves you so much! Keep those anchor

---

[36] *Cambridge Dictionary*, Cambridge University Press, "Anchor", 2022, https://dictionary.cambridge.org/us/dictionary/english/anchor
[37] James 1:6-8 (NKJV).

ropes of faith, trust, hope, and love in good condition through prayer, Bible study, and communion with other Christians. Like the red mylar balloon, you can attract the attention of others. Only, with God's help, you will be attracting their attention to your anchor, Jesus Christ, our Lord and Savior.

Footprints of Discipleship

"The LORD directs the steps of the godly.
He delights in every detail of their lives."[38]

This morning I read a devotional by Max Lucado entitled "Footprints of Discipleship" which brought many thoughts to mind. Max writes:

"In our faith we follow in someone's steps. A parent, a teacher, a hero – none of us is the first to walk the trail. All of us have someone we follow.

In our faith we leave footprints to guide others. A child, a friend, a recent convert. None should be left to walk the trail alone.

It's the principle of discipleship."[39]

After reading these words, my first thought of "following in someone's footprints" was of our older son, John, helping his daddy cut the grass. I remember the scene just like it was yesterday. John loved following his daddy around the yard and the house to "help" him. One day he had pulled his toy lawn mower outside, and I saw him cutting grass just like Mike was doing. He was a safe distance

---

[38] Psalm 37:23 (NLT).
[39] Max Lucado, *Grace for the Moment*, (Tennessee: Thomas Nelson, 2007), March 29.

from Mike, and in his mind, he was helping his daddy take care of the yard. It was such a cute scene to watch!

Think of the impact that each "following in someone's footprints" has on the next generation. You and I followed someone around, and that someone and others we followed made many impressions on us, guided us along our life's pathway, and taught us important matters about how to live our lives. Even now, there are people who impact my life and challenge me in ways that inspire me to be more "like Christ."

As Max writes, "none of us is the first to walk the trail. All of us have someone we follow." At some point in our lifetime, we had a question to answer about the person(s) we were following: Is this the right person to follow? Is this person teaching me and leading me to a righteous life in Christ? Is this person leading me into trouble and the wrong path in life?

Yes, our son was following and copying what his daddy was doing. This is how we learn best – by seeing, hearing, and doing. Now, our granddaughter is "following" him and her mom. She is copying her parents in things such as drinking out of a mug. She sees them doing this in the mornings, and she wants to drink her water out of a mug as well. This is how we learn.

May we be assured that we are following in the right footprints – God's Footprints of Discipleship – as we maneuver this life He is leading us through!

God's Everlasting Love

> "I am the Holy One living among you,
> and I will not come to destroy.
> For someday the people will follow me."[40]

Raising children is greatly filled with ups and downs – the days that you wish would end sooner and those you wish would last forever. However, when the children reach 18 years of age, you feel like you have accomplished something! At least Mike and I did. We believed that we had taught our boys all that we knew to teach them at the time, but certainly we made a lot of mistakes along the way. And yes, there are things we wish we had done differently or spent more time teaching, but we felt like at 18 years of age, they would be able to make their own decisions. When each of them went to college, Mike and I gave them "the talk."

When they reached 18, we had taught them as much as we could, but then it was time for them to learn to make their own decisions (and mistakes) *and* accept the consequences that followed – good or not so good. We stressed that we would always be there for them if they needed to talk things through or get some advice. We also told them that we loved them and would *always* love them regardless of their acts. We may not agree with their actions or words, but we would always love them. So off they each went to Charlotte and then

---

[40] Hosea 11:9-10 (NLT).

to Raleigh 2 years later. (And believe me, it wasn't as simple as this reads. Ya'll know what I'm talking about!!)

In my reading from the prophets in the Old Testament (OT), I have seen how God has taken this same approach with us, but He revealed this to me this morning – the concept of a deep and everlasting love.

Hosea gave us God's words on how He was ready to destroy Israel (again!) because of its sins against Him. How many times have I read this in the OT and wondered "How, God, can you keep loving us when your people turn away?" These verses in Chapter 11 below describe what I'm talking about:

> "For my people are determined to desert me. They call me the Most High,
>> but they don't truly honor me.
>
> "Oh, how can I give you up, Israel? How can I let you go?
> How can I destroy you like Admah or demolish you like Zeboiim?
> My heart is torn within me, and my compassion overflows.
> No, I will not unleash my fierce anger. I will not completely destroy Israel,
> for I am God and not a mere mortal. I am the Holy One living among you,
> and I will not come to destroy.
> For someday the people will follow me. I, the Lord, will roar like a lion.
> And when I roar, my people will return trembling from the west." [41]

God has given us every chance in the world to turn back to Him, and thankfully, many of us have!! And I do believe that hundreds of

---

[41] Hosea 11:7-10a (NLT).

thousands more are turning to Him every day. Praise God for those who are ministering to others to show them our God!

But deep down, He reveals how He still loves His people. Many of us know that parenting is not an easy responsibility in life. However, God has led our parents/other family members to teach us His ways. He knows that we will learn to live on our own and make our own decisions, but will He agree with all of these decisions? No. He gave us free will to choose our path every day and make decisions. He obviously wants us to consult Him first, but that doesn't always happen.

Nevertheless, if we have the right relationship with God, then we know without a doubt that He will still love us even if we take the wrong path. All we have to do is tell Him, "I am sorry, God. That was wrong," and He will continue to shower His love and guidance on us. He will forget our sins.

> "I – yes, I alone – will blot out your sins for my own sake and will never think of them again."[42]

By using God as our "Father" example, we learn to teach our children in His ways and still love them when they do wrong. There are many reasons why they do wrong, and it most certainly tries our patience; however if we take the time to talk to them about it, they will usually share, and it becomes a teaching moment. I believe that this is how God used His prophets - to share His words and warnings with His people in order to teach them what to do to return to Him and His love. Whether or not they accepted this or learned from it was up to them.

The Bible teaches us so much, but it has taken me this year to hear what God is saying to me about His words in the Old Testament through the reading of the One Year Bible. Ask for God to reveal His meanings to you and to reveal his words as they are applicable to our generation.

---

[42] Isaiah 43:25 (NLT).

By the way, our boys learned a lot during college and are still learning as we all are. With a beautiful granddaughter close by and 2 grandsons on the way in 2022, I look forward to seeing the teachings they will receive from our sons and their wives. I also am so grateful for the teachings from my parents and their parents and the generations before them as God's Word has been handed down to each of us.

God's Best Nutrition Plan Ever!

"Let the [spoken] word of Christ have its home within you [dwelling in your heart and mind—permeating every aspect of your being] as you teach [spiritual things] *and* admonish *and* train one another with all wisdom, singing psalms and hymns and spiritual songs with thankfulness in your hearts to God."[43]

Over the years, I have often wondered how magazines, blogs, commercials, and online reviews are able to create articles on new diets and new exercise plans every year! In the fall, they will have the *best plan ever* for how not to overeat at Thanksgiving or Christmas. After the New Year, they will have the *best plan ever* to match your diet with your new gym workout program to prep for spring and summer. In the spring, they will have the *best plan ever* for your swimsuit wear for the summer. In the summer, they will have the *best plan ever* for staying fit. And then they will do it again the next year!! How do they keep producing the *best plan ever* year after year?

If these plans really worked, most women (and men) would be slimmer, have a flat belly, have shed 2 or 3 sizes, and just plain have a "hot body"! Do you see them in your town? Maybe some, but really look! If most women and men looked better, these magazines wouldn't have a need for these articles. But there is obviously a section of the magazine market which thrives on these various diets

---

[43] Colossians 3:16 (AMP).

and exercise plans, and these people keep looking for just the right one. It must be so frustrating!!

Certainly, we want our daily intake of food to be full of nutrients, which we need for growth and good health. Sometimes we even need nutritional supplements as advised by our doctors. But the bottom line is that we need to put healthy foods into our bodies and keep active in order to keep vibrant and energetic! This is easier said than done, but I try! After all, I do like my sweets!

However, I know someone who has the ultimate, *best nutrition plan ever* – our awesome God who created us!

His plan is for life eternal. It includes divine thoughts on which to focus our minds, daily Bible nuggets from His Word, and talks with Him about what is bothering us or what we love about Him.

His plan never wavers. His plan fits all, regardless of where we are on this road of life, and His plan will never change. He will always be with us to encourage us, guide us, challenge us, and answer our questions.

Recently I was reading the "Jesus Calling" devotional book, and this sentence grabbed my attention. "As My Face shines upon you, you receive nutrients that enhance your growth in grace."[44]

I had not thought about using the word "nutrients" to describe what we receive from Jesus to enhance our growth. A nutrient is something that promotes our growth, provides energy, and keeps our physical bodies living. When we are in God's presence, He gives us nutrients. He doesn't just give us what we *want*. He gives us what is *required* and crucial to the growth and sustenance of our faith-filled lives.

But the end of the sentence states "enhance your growth in grace". What is our "growth in grace"?

> "2 Peter 3:18 tells us to 'grow in the grace and knowledge of the Lord Jesus Christ.' To grow in grace is to mature as a Christian. We grow in grace

---

[44] Young, Sarah, *Jesus Calling*, (Tennessee, Thomas Nelson, 2011), 261.

by reading God's Word and letting it 'dwell in us richly' (Colossians 3:16) and by praying. Those actions by themselves don't mature us, but God uses these spiritual disciplines to help us grow."[45]

This is that amazing grace which we don't deserve, but God has saved us with it. We can and will mature as Christians if we follow His *best nutrition plan ever.*

1. There will be no need to be discouraged before you even start. God's mercies "begin afresh each morning."[46]
2. There will be no need to think you are all alone in this. God loves community!
3. There will be no need to look for new plans every season. God never changes!

I encourage you to give God's plan a try!

---

[45] "What Does it Mean to Grow in Grace", Got Questions, updated January 4, 2022, https://www.gotquestions.org/grow-in-grace.html
[46] Lamentations 3:23 (NLT).

Hangin' On By a Thread or Two Hands?

> "When troubles of any kind come your way,
> consider it an opportunity for great joy. For you
> know that when your faith is tested,
> your endurance has a chance to grow."[47]

Recently, we had some really strong winds overnight, and the majority of the leaves on our silver maple tree were on the ground by the next morning. Notice I wrote the *majority* of the leaves were on the ground. My view showed 8-10 leaves still attached to a few branches. And not only that but they still retained their beautiful colors of green, red, and yellow.

While using the elliptical machine over the past several days, I have been watching these leaves. These beauties with their vibrant colors are still hanging on the tree!

Now how did that happen? Hundreds of leaves are on the ground – covering the ground so the grass is not visible – but a few stubborn or sturdy ones are still on the tree.

After a few minutes of investigating, I learned why some leaves do not drop right away:

> As winter approaches, tree leaves stop producing chlorophyll. At that point, the branches also begin to develop their "abscission" cells. These are cells that scissor off the dying leaves and seal up the stem

---

[47] James 1:2-3 (NLT).

attachments. But if the weather drops early in a sudden cold snap, it can kill the leaves immediately. This takes the leaf color directly from green to brown. It also prevents the development of the abscission tissue. This essentially means the leaves are not scissored off the branches but instead remain attached. Don't worry, your tree will be fine. The leaves will fall at some point, and new leaves will grow in normally the following spring.[48]

The dropping of leaves is a natural process of preparing for winter. God made these trees to know how and when to protect themselves during the year. As the branches cut off the dying leaves, they seal up the stem attachment for the winter. This protection ensures the new bud for next spring. So here we go, God! What is the spiritual side of this?

First of all, what does the phrase "hanging on" bring to mind?

- hanging on to my mother's dresses as a young child and hiding behind her because I was so shy
- hanging on to keepsakes from Mom's memorial service which are still on my desk
- hanging on to our boys' school papers and awards and wondering what to do with them
- hanging on to tree branches and swinging like a monkey

"Hangin' on" can be a positive or negative phrase depending on what is happening in your life at any given time. When we are "hangin' on" in the difficulties of life, we need to remember that God has not left us. He is not tending to someone else's problems & forgetting ours. Remember that He is omniscient – "having infinite

---

[48] Ted Spengler, "Tree Leaves Didn't Drop in Winter: Reasons Why Leaves Did Not Drop Off A Tree", updated September 1. 2020, https://www.gardeningknowhow.com/ornamental/trees/tgen/why-leaves-did-not-fall-off-tree.htm

awareness, understanding, and insight"[49] and omnipresent – "present everywhere at the same time"[50]. He alone knows what is happening in your life!

God will ensure that these leaves will fall at just the right time, but for now, he is giving me the beauty of His colors to gaze on a while longer as the rest of the landscape begins to change to brown and tan.

> "For I know the plans I have for you," says the LORD.
> "They are plans for good and not for disaster, to give you a future and a hope."[51]

He will do the same for you. He will help you to hang on regardless of the circumstances. Just as the tree is still preparing for winter and the buds for next spring, He is preparing us for each day. He knows the plans He has for us, and He will guide us through those plans as long as we continue to hang on. It doesn't matter whether we are hanging by a thread or with full grips from both hands. He is here to support and guide us.

Even our two dogwood trees have a plan. They already have buds while it is the fall of the year.

> "A bud is a tree's way of getting a leaf or flower through the winter. When it's too cold and water is locked up in ice, plants can't grow. But even in a cold-winter climate, woody plants can get a head start on

---

[49] *Merriam-Webster Dictionary*, "Omniscient", https://www.merriam-webster.com/dictionary/omniscient.
[50] *Merriam-Webster Dictionary*, "Omnipresent", https://www.dictionary.com/browse/omnipresent.
[51] Jeremiah 29:11 (NLT).

next year by forming buds while it's still warm and then pausing their growth until spring."[52]

At some time, the colors will fade; the leaves will fall; the tree will look dormant through the winter, but then spring comes. However, the tree is not dormant. There is an entire underground system among the roots of all trees which protect them, feed them, and prepare them for the next stage or season. These trees are preparing for spring and new growth.

God is doing the same in each of us. He is preparing us for the plans He has for us – for now and for the future. So, keep hangin' on!

---

[52] Beth Botts, "Even in winter, buds help woody plants get a start on spring", www.gardeningknowhow.com, Chicago Tribune, December 3, 2018, https://www.chicagotribune.com/lifestyles/home-and-garden/ct-life-1216-garden-morton-20181203-story.html,

Hold On!

"Why are you so afraid? Do you still have no faith?"[53]

Have you ever experienced a hurricane? I have not, but I have experienced something similar. When vacationing on the Outer Banks, NC, Mike and I were in the middle of a nor'easter which came through at full throttle. The winds were at least 26 mph with gusts up to 50 mph! I simply can't imagine being hunkered down in a cottage with a hurricane blowing through at 75+ mph!

The cottage we were staying in was moving slightly with the larger gusts. I was at the table working on a jigsaw puzzle, feeling my chair and the table move. Oh my!!! This actually reminded me of a get-away several years ago when Mike and I spent a Valentine's weekend at Emerald Isle. It was the first time we had experienced a nor'easter at the beach. We were on the upstairs floor lying in bed and wide awake. The bed was shaking, and the house was moving. Mike reminded both of us that this was exactly what the house was built to do – move with the gusts. Sleep was hard to come by that night!

I continued to think about that experience as I worked on the puzzle. I wasn't fearful, but it was a little unnerving. Mark 4:35-41 came to mind. Jesus had told the disciples that they would be crossing the sea to the other side, and He went to sleep. Meanwhile a "furious squall came up".[54] It was so violent that they had to wake

---

[53] Mark 4:40 (NIV).
[54] Mark 4:37 (NIV).

Jesus to come help them. He calmed the sea and asked why they still had no faith.

Faith. The one word that defines our relationship with Jesus. Either we have it or we don't. If we don't, then we are likely to drown in those waves crashing over the boat. How can we survive the storms of life without faith in Jesus? How can we help others in the community of Christ without faith in Jesus? How can we fulfill God's purpose for our lives without faith in Jesus?

I don't believe we can. Maybe we can get by somehow, but how effective will we be without Jesus in our lives? How can we demonstrate Jesus to others if we don't have faith?

The storms will come; the pain is real; the unfairness is overwhelming. It doesn't stop regardless of how hard we scream or yell!

Just remember this: When the very core of your being feels like it is swaying and being rocked off its foundation, *just hold on*. You have to hold on to God and believe. That is called faith.

Hold on to the Rock of your foundation.
In Jesus' Name, I pray!

He Promised

"I am holding you by your right hand—I, the
Lord your God—and I say to you,
Don't be afraid; I am here to help you."[55]

There are numerous promises which God has made to His people. The Bible is filled with them throughout the Old and New Testaments. Some of these Promises include:

- Salvation
- Comfort in our trials
- Things which work out for our good
- Always being with us
- Protection
- His love that never fails

It's almost hard to stop listing!

This morning as I went on my short walk around the neighborhood, I saw something that gave me hope for cooler weather in the months to come. A red dogwood leaf!

For me, this is the Promise of a new season coming:

- a season to bring a change in the landscape
- a season to show His variety of colors
- a season to bring the cooler breezes and temperatures

---

[55] Isaiah 41:13 (TLB).

- a season to bring new life and vitality to each of us after these continuous 90+ degree temperatures which make it hard to breathe
- a season to return to studying His Word in an instructional setting, such as Sunday School or a Bible study group or church
- a season to begin afresh in His Word

As much as I would love wearing my shorts and T-shirts year-round, I cannot imagine living where there is no change in the seasons. I am one who loves "change" in certain areas of my life – daily tasks/events, restaurants, seasons, projects. Living the "same" every day becomes uninteresting for me which translates into my brain being less stimulated.

However, God Promised! And I knew when I saw that red leaf that I was seeing one of His Promises. The seasons *will* change. His love will *never* change. He will comfort us in our daily trials. His Will is best for us. He will protect us. He will always be with us. He alone can offer us salvation for an eternal life with Him.

What more can we ask for? Why should we worry? He Promised!!

How Do You Water Your Soul and Spirit?

"But those who drink the water I give will never be thirsty again. It becomes a fresh, bubbling spring within them, giving them eternal life."[56]

While eating breakfast, I watched a video on tips for watering hanging baskets. As the expert reviewed these 3 tips, I thought about the Living Waters of scripture and the verse above describing the water that Jesus gives as "a fresh, bubbling spring." We will never be thirsty again when we drink this water.

We "water" our souls and spirits by reading the Word of God. Let's consider what these three tips for watering plants would look like through spiritual eyes.[57]

<u>Tip #1: Water Adequately</u>: *"Learn how heavy the plant needs to be when water is needed. Only water until it is adequate. If you have hanging baskets, lift the basket to determine the water content. The water requirements may change from day to day."*

It has been my experience that the scriptures are opened to me more easily at certain times than others.

---

[56] John 4:14 (NLT).
[57] Scott Sharkey, "How to Properly Water Hanging Baskets", www.beatyourneighbor.com, July 8, 2022, https://beatyourneighbor.com/how-to-videos/

Since I am sensitive to the structure and grammar of sentences, I sometimes have trouble understanding the grammar used and how the sentence should be read. Trying to maneuver through these scriptures is like bearing a weight that slows me down, and I can only absorb a smaller number of scriptures. This is not the time for me to try to read too much.

At other times, the scriptures and study notes give so much enlightenment that I can't stop reading! That is when I want more and more Living Water, which will nourish the spring within me!

<u>Tip #2: 24-hour Mentality</u>: *"We should water just enough for the roots to be nourished during a 24-hour period."*

Determining that amount comes with practice. I have heard over the years that a plant should be watered until the water is dripping from the bottom of the pot. This video source today stated that this is not true. That idea would be like drinking 5 gallons of water at a time, which our bodies cannot handle. The same would be true with a plant – it can't handle an overabundance of water.

Spiritually, is there such a thing as getting too much of the Word of God? Can we become inundated with the Word of God? Speaking in a general sense, I believe we cannot get too much of God's Word, but the frequency & quantity do matter to me. When I am preparing for my Sunday School class, I might spend 1-2 hours for a few days trying to research and read the scriptures we are discussing. But there comes a time when I am "done"! My brain simply cannot receive any more information at that time. It is like the plant which is being given too much "water". If I were to continue, the scriptures and meanings would flow right through me without being absorbed in my mind or my spirit. My brain, like a plant, must have time to realize the meanings of the scriptures/research and to plan the presentation to my group. I need just enough, which comes with practice each week.

Tip #3: Water in the morning: *"The best time to water plants is in the morning."*

I know that, but I have always loved being in the yard after supper, especially before I retired. After supper is still my favorite time to water, but I have learned that watering at that time day after day can slowly "kill" the plant. The water soaks into the soil/roots overnight when there is no means for drying. If the roots stay wet, they will eventually rot. By watering in the morning, the roots can more easily absorb the water and send nutrients to the plant as it dries throughout the day.

Since retirement, I have come to enjoy my time with God in the morning. I'm not an early morning person so it was difficult to do this when preparing for work. After we moved to Clarksville, I remember asking a friend about this. Does it matter if we have "God Time" in the evening versus the morning? She simply answered that God was happy to have the time with me when it worked best for me. It wasn't a matter of when but a matter of doing it that was important. Now it works best in the morning since it prepares me for the day and gives me God's teachings to think about during the day. Of course, there are days when it doesn't happen. Like today, He has me writing His message, given to me while eating breakfast!

Consider how you water your soul and spirit. Do you water adequately in the morning actively considering the likely needs of the plants for the next 24 hours? We must learn to take as much care for our reading of God's Word as we do our beautiful plants.

God, we thank you for all of your creation and what it teaches us! Help us to keep ourselves watered just enough for today.

How's Your Prayer Life?

> "But you are a chosen people, a royal priesthood, a holy nation, God's special possession, that you may declare the praises of him who called you out of darkness into his wonderful light."[58]

I believe that when we pray, God isn't watching the positions we place ourselves in during our prayer time but focuses on our prayers and relationships with him. This devotional by Cindy Trimm brought this to mind.

> "God will speak to each of us in different ways, and the way God speaks to one person can be markedly different from the way He speaks to another. God isn't interested in getting us to learn rules and requirements and living life merely by following the dictates of a rulebook. He wants us to come to Him that we might know Him for ourselves. He wants a unique relationship with each of us just as He created each of us as unique individuals. God is all about relationship, and the key to it is masterful prayer."[59]

---

[58] 1 Peter 2:9 (NIV).
[59] Cindy Trimm, *Commanding Your Morning Daily Devotional* (Lake Mary, FL, Charisma House, 2014), 347.

Recently I drove to a meeting about 30 minutes away, and I'll have to say that I was looking forward to driving alone. Those are some of the most precious times for me to commune with God, and this day was no exception. I was in prayer the entire time - praying for the meeting, the leader, every person there, the mission of this meeting, and other situations on my heart. By the time I arrived, my entire body and mind were at peace and joyful. Oh, how God works!!

Yet I must tell you that it is very difficult for me to pray for that length of time (or any time longer than 5-10 minutes) at home. What is that all about? I am praying to the same God in a quiet house in my prayer/study corner. Well, I believe the answer is the environment which is different. In my house there are all sorts of distractions - work to be done piled around my desk, cleaning that is needed when I see the dust on the desk in our bedroom, food that needs to be cooked in the kitchen, and don't even let me go in the family room where the TV is showing football!! When I am driving, God has removed all of the distractions of everyday life.

What about the time of day when you pray? I used to only have purposeful prayer time with God late at night and felt that was wrong because everything one reads about prayer time tells us to pray in the morning when we arise. And I get that! It makes perfect sense to begin the day that way, but it wasn't happening for me. However, since beginning this blog, mornings have become precious times for me (as long as the house is quiet!) because I do some of my writing and enjoy my God-time then. God can change us!

I shall continue this journey of talking with God throughout the day and having that purposeful prayer time when it is right for God and me. He is always open and available - 24/7 - to hear from us, his precious sons, priests, and lords.

Let's continue the unique relationship that each of us has with God. He must certainly love variety because he made each of us distinctive and marvelous!! Keep the light shining in yourself for others!!!

I Wasn't Created to Bear It Alone

"Fear not, for I *am* with you;
Be not dismayed, for I *am* your God.
I will strengthen you,
Yes, I will help you,
I will uphold you with My righteous right hand."[60]

Today when I was traveling to a friend's house, these words "popped" at me from the song playing on the radio. God perked my ears to these words:

"*I wasn't created to bear it alone*"[61]

Can you relate to this? Yes, this is one of those nuggets which is sharing nothing new with you but has woken up something in me that makes me want to say "God, you did this for me?" You made it impossible for me to carry any load on my own without You. Thank You, God!

In his infinite wisdom, God created us, *from the very beginning of time*, to come to Him with every burden; every care; every good thing; every new discovery; every *THING*. He never intended us to go through life alone or to go through life without Him!

Is it our pride that makes us think we can handle things ourselves?

---

[60] Isaiah 41:10 (NKJV).
[61] Carnes, Cody. "Run to the Father", July 26, 2019, #3 on *Run to the Father* album, Essential Music Publishing, 2019.

Let me speak for myself. Years ago, I thought that I should be able to figure out how to solve my problems. That was part of being a mature adult, right? The ones I couldn't solve were the ones I could take to God. He seemed really good with the BIG problems. Let's just say that I don't think that way anymore. Praise God!

I know that I should/do go to God with every situation, regardless of whether it is a problem or a praise. (He should receive our thanks as well as our help requests!) Since we live in a fallen world, it goes to reason that we will always need help – divine help named Jesus!

God wants us to run to Him again and again. We won't wear out the path or bother Him. He is always available! Isaiah 41:10 tells us that He is always with us and will strengthen us and help us. What more do we need other than this promise from God?

God does not want and never intended for us to "bear it alone", whatever the "it" is. He is always here to help us. He may send a friend or a stranger with a word. He may direct us to see things with our spiritual eyes instead of our natural eyes. He may put a certain book in our hands to read. He may direct someone to send that special postcard with just the right scripture on it. God's ways are endless, but *HE WILL BE WITH US SO WE DO NOT HAVE TO BEAR IT ALONE!*

Believe this. Put your faith in this. Trust His Word. Trust Him! There is no one else.

Is There Hope for These Dry Bones/Healing of the Nation

> "Then you, my people, will know that I am the LORD, when I open your graves and bring you up from them. I will put my Spirit in you and you will live, and I will settle you in your own land. Then you will know that I the LORD have spoken, and I have done it, declares the LORD."[62]

The verses of Ezekiel 37:1-14 are some of my favorites in the Old Testament. They convey the story of the Israelites and their future through a vision which God gave to Ezekiel. The Israelites were a broken people. They were in captivity in Babylon. They had become lost, despondent, confused, and hopeless. They saw no end in sight for ever making it back to their own land. Many would say that this describes today's world. I think some believers are uncertain about our own future. It appears to be a future with no hope in sight for our country ever returning to God.

Here is a description of the captivity of the Israelites by the Babylonians.

> "But the captivity did not bring the people of Judah back to God. This judgment of God only seemed to drive the people into greater wickedness. They

---

[62] Ezekiel 37:13-14 (NIV).

worshiped idols and set up shrines in the hills and defiled the sanctuary of Jehovah (Ezekiel 5:11). They had been wicked and stiff-necked; they were guilty of unspeakable sin and abomination. When other nations did what Israel had done, God wiped them out... But all of God's dealings with Israel were for correction. He was punishing his children for their sin and was teaching them great lessons. He said a remnant would survive."[63]

How far away from God has our nation of today strayed? How many have been "wicked and stiff-necked"?

In these verses, God has taken Ezekiel (in a vision) to a deserted land where all he can see are dry bones which are not connected to each other but are lying flat on the ground as far as he can see - even into other countries! God commanded Ezekiel to prophesy to these bones and tell them to "hear (emphasis mine) the word of the Lord."[64] The word <u>hear</u> is *shama'* (shaw-mah') in Hebrew, and it means to hear intelligently and be attentive.[65] God didn't just want them to listen to this command, and let the words go in one ear and out the other. He intended for them to be attentive and to hear these words with understanding. He meant business.

There was a noise, a shaking that took place, a quaking, a rattling. **God's Word** had stirred these bones into action, and the healing process had begun. The sinews connected the bones, and the skin covered them, but there was no breath. God commanded Ezekiel to prophesy to the wind, or *ruwach* meaning breath,[66] to come upon the slain that they might live. Upon Ezekiel's word, the breath came into

---

[63] Mears, Dr. Henrietta C., *What the Bible is All About*; (California, Regal Books, 1953), 259-260, 262

[64] Ezekiel 37:4 (NIV).

[65] Strong, James, *Strong's Expanded Exhaustive Concordance of the Bible*, (Tennessee, Thomas Nelson, 2001), 285.

[66] Strong, James, *Strong's Expanded Exhaustive Concordance of the Bible*, (Tennessee, Thomas Nelson, 2001), 258-259.

these reconnected bones covered with skin, and they lived. The word *live* is *chayah* (khaw-yaw) which means to recover; repair; restore to life.[67] They stood up on their feet and were an exceeding great army!

But that's not the end of this vision.

The Lord continued to talk with Ezekiel explaining that these bones represented the whole house of Israel. The Israelites had said that their bones were dry, and their hope was lost, but that is **not what God said.** God told Ezekiel to prophesy once again to them that he would open their graves and bring them out. He would put **His Spirit** in them and place them in their own land, and they would know that it was the Lord who performed it.

Through this summary of the "dry bones" scripture, God was showing Ezekiel how he was going to bring back together the people of Israel - to reconnect them; restore them; give them hope; let them know without a doubt that he was their God. He needed Ezekiel to help the Israelites understand this. With as many times as God's people turned away from him, He continued to use various ways to bring them back to Him. He could have wiped them out, but He loved them too much and wanted them to know that He would never give up on them.

This Old Testament God is still in control now. Our God is bigger than anything that is happening in this earthly world! As Ezekiel prophesied to the bones, they heard God's Word. God wants His people to hear Him now - to reconnect, repair, heal, and revive. He will cover us with His Almighty Word and the blood of Jesus to launch this process of reconnecting and recovering. Then He will put **His Spirit** in us and place us in the right locations for His purpose, and all peoples will know that it is the Lord who is performing it. No one else is capable of this.

We must remember God's promises in His Word and not what the "other guy" said nor how we "feel". May we continue to keep our focus on God and not be distracted by the enemy or the evening

---

[67] Strong, James, *Strong's Expanded Exhaustive Concordance of the Bible*, (Tennessee, Thomas Nelson, 2001), 86.

news or social media. Yes, we need to stay informed, but we do not need to be consumed with it.

Let God do what He does best – to love and take care of us. He knows how. He has a pretty good track record. He needs us to be patient! But we MUST believe in Him, trust in Him, and have faith that He knows best. He will perform it.

Jesus, the Bread of Life: How Far Would You Go To Get It?

"He who believes in Me shall never thirst.[68]"

I don't know about you, but I absolutely LOVE bread! All kinds of homemade bread and especially right out of the oven or bread maker! The smells are extraordinarily wonderful as well as the taste! Yummm... When thinking about this, I began reading John 6, Jesus as the Bread of Life. As this section begins, throngs of people were looking for Jesus after being fed with the twelve loaves and fishes and went across the sea to find him in Capernaum. He recognized that they had put forth the effort to find him, and he said to them:

> "...'Most assuredly, I say to you, you seek Me, not because you saw the signs, but because you ate of the loaves and were filled. Do not labor for the food which perishes, but for the food which endures to everlasting life, which the Son of Man will give you, because God the Father has set His seal on Him.'"[69]

Jesus knew that they had sought after him because of the Word he had taught, and they wanted to know more.

Do you ever wonder how hard you would try and how far you

---

[68] John 6:35 (NKJV).
[69] John 6:26–27 (NKJV).

would go to hear the Word of God? Travel was not as easy in Jesus' day as it is today. In fact, it's like comparing apples to oranges. When we lived in Durham, NC, we attended a ministry in Henderson, NC, which was 50 minutes from our house. When people asked where we attended church and we told them, they thought we had moved to Henderson. They couldn't understand why we traveled so far to attend church. Sure, there were times when we dragged our feet, but those were few. We also have a neighbor now who travels back to Durham at least twice a week to worship in their church there. I think you will do what you have to do if the truth of the Word is being taught.

Verse 27 reads: "Do not labor for the food which perishes."

Jesus told the people not to waste their time on "meat" which perished or turned bad. That type of meat was what we ate in the natural within a set number of days or it would spoil. It would only satisfy us for an hour or two. Then we would be looking for something else to eat. What should we eat?

The last part of verse 27 answers that question. We should eat "the food which endures to everlasting life", which is God's Word. "Labor" in the Greek means to toil or commit to.[70] We have to work hard to get it, but it will "endure"[71], which means to stay, abide, dwell, remain. We won't feel empty in an hour or two after consuming this Word, the bread of life. But we will be hungry for more of it! The more we consume the Word of God, the stronger our physical bodies (God's temple) will be, and the more knowledgeable our minds will be when filled with scripture, which is a means of fending off the enemy!

---

[70] Strong, James, Strong's Expanded Exhaustive Concordance of the Bible, (Tennessee, Thomas Nelson, 2001), 102.

[71] Strong, James, Strong's Expanded Exhaustive Concordance of the Bible, (Tennessee, Thomas Nelson, 2001), 160.

"And Jesus said to them, "I am the bread of life. He who comes to Me shall never hunger, and he who believes in Me shall never thirst.""[72]

When you **come** to Jesus and **believe** in him, you shall never be spiritually hungry or thirsty again! This is the bread that I want! How about you?

---

[72] John 6:35 (NKJV).

The Joy of a Babe

"And the ransomed of the Lord shall return, And come to Zion with singing,
With everlasting joy on their heads. They shall obtain joy and gladness, And sorrow and sighing shall flee away."[73]

Yesterday we lit the Advent candle for JOY. The scripture above was the reading. With "everlasting joy"…that is some kind of joy! It will never end. This prompted me to think about the most joyous occasions in my life. There are so many, and they lifted my spirit as high as I thought it could go, but then in October 2020, we found out that we were going to be grandparents in May of 2021. What a game-changer for my spirit! Many of you know what I mean.

We met John and Jess (our older son and his wife) for dinner one night and greeted each other in the parking lot. Then John handed us a note card from Darcy and Huxley, our sweet granddogs. I couldn't imagine why they were sending us a card. We had not sent them anything recently, had we? As these thoughts went through my mind, I opened the card. Mike and I read it. My heart started beating faster, and I said "What is this? Baby West in May 2021???? Wait…what??" Mike and I had to read it twice to be sure of what we read. Oh, the joy which still fills my heart!

Joy means a "state of happiness, the prospect of possessing what

---

[73] Isaiah 35:10 (NKJV).

one desires, and the expression or exhibition of such emotion." Some synonyms include "elatedness, exhilaration, exultation, ecstasy."[74] I know these were the emotions I was feeling. There is so much joy surrounding a baby. Don't our hearts just melt?

Do we feel that same JOY thinking of the birth of Jesus? I began wondering about Mary, the mother of Jesus. What was she feeling? Nervous? Joyful? Wondering how to tell Joseph and her parents and Joseph's parents? What to tell her best friend? How in the world to explain her mixture of emotions? We don't really know the answers to these questions, but we do know that she rejoiced as seen in Luke 1:46-48. We know that she humbly accepted the word of the Lord from Gabriel.

What about Joseph? Was it Joy? Was it unbelief that his betrothed was pregnant and by whom? I recently read this from "Devotions Daily – Joseph's Heartbreak: God Speaks Into Sorrow":

> "...my heart aches for Joseph. I wonder what his dreams looked like before his life took such a hairpin turn. Had he dreamt of the love he would share with Mary or about the night he would make her his own? Had he imagined their children, their home, or the secrets they would whisper in the dark? Joseph was a real man with real dreams, and I would imagine that at this moment in his life, those long-held desires lay in ruins around his feet. Nothing was going the way he had imagined it would go."[75]

The angel of the Lord visited Joseph in a dream and explained what was happening. He then rose and took Mary as his wife. So yes,

---

[74] *Merriam-Webster Dictionary*, "Joy", https://www.merriam-webster.com/dictionary/joy

[75] Bo Stern, "Joseph's Heartbreak: God Speaks into Sorrow", www.Faithgateway.com, Harper Collins Christian Publishing, 2020, https://faithgateway.com/blogs/christian-books/josephs-heartbreak-god-speaks-sorrow

it all came about differently from what each of them had planned, but God used them to bring JOY to the world in the form of Jesus.

Regardless of how these parents felt, they were assured that God was behind this. God made this decision to come to earth as a human, as a baby. What responsibility Mary and Joseph had on their shoulders!

But how was this baby received? With incredible joy and thanksgiving to God!

> "Now when they had seen *Him,* they made widely known the saying which was told them concerning this Child. And all those who heard *it* marveled at those things which were told them by the shepherds. But Mary kept all these things and pondered *them* in her heart. Then the shepherds returned, glorifying and praising God for all the things that they had heard and seen, as it was told them."[76]

There is just something about the birth of a baby which stirs and melts our hearts. Now think about the Joy of the birth of Jesus. All heaven rejoiced as well as those surrounding them at the manger. The wonderful, ecstatic, elated feeling of Joy was present and will always be present for those who Believe. This kind of Joy is everlasting because our God and His love are everlasting.

Let us celebrate the birth of this babe known as Jesus who grew to become the ultimate sacrifice for us. That is something to be Joyful and Grateful for!

---

[76] Luke 2:17-20 (NKJV).

Only the best doggie grandparents get promoted to human grandparents!
Baby West Due May 2021

♡ Huxley & Darcy

The Roar of Spittin' Rain

> "All the earth worships you and sings praises to you;
> they sing praises to your name."[77]

I had just arrived home from exercising at the YMCA. I knew we were supposed to get a brief shower of rain around 3:00pm. When I left the car, I felt a "spittin' rain" falling, but as I walked past the black plastic covering the ground next to the driveway, I could hear the rain falling as if it were magnified!

I was amazed at how loud the "spittin' rain" sounded on that plastic. Do you know what I'm talking about? Something that I would never have given another thought about suddenly became loud to my senses.

What came into my spirit was the volume of sound which can come from the **combination** of many small, soft voices! As we pray to God, dance for God, sing for God, raise our hands to God, let's do it with many people who love God!! And as we do, we know that the volume will reach the heavens, and our praises will be pleasing to the God who loves us and cares so much for us!!

This doesn't mean that our individual sharing times with God are not pleasing to Him or are not heard. He adores every word we utter to Him, every minute we spend with Him, and every burden we share with Him. These personal times are the ones which develop our own unique relationship with God.

---

[77] Psalm 66:4 (ESV).

But consider the effects of the **combination** of voices in various arenas in life. Just think about the volume of voices at March Madness college basketball games! How often we yell in excitement or frustration during the game! It is one thing to hear this in one's own home, but it is entirely another to hear it in a 20,000-seat arena! A resounding roar!

Can you imagine praising God in this way? Our youth went to WinterJam in Raleigh, NC recently. This is Christian music's biggest multi-artist tour and was held at PNC Arena, which has a capacity of 19,722. What a way to praise God by joining others in singing and yelling and using their individual voices. What a **roar** of voices! That's what I call lifting a praise for God!

Think on these scriptures which encourage us, and even instruct us, to praise God together. Our individual, small voices combined in song and prayer will no doubt reach God with a loud **roar** – a very pleasing roar!!

> "Through him then let us continually offer up a sacrifice of praise to God, that is, the fruit of lips that acknowledge his name."[78]

> "Oh come, let us sing to the LORD; let us make a joyful noise to the rock of our salvation!"[79]

> "I will praise the name of God with a song; I will magnify him with thanksgiving."[80]

Keep roaring for God!

---

[78] Hebrews 13:15 (ESV).
[79] Psalm 95:1 (ESV).
[80] Psalm 69:30 (ESV).

Matters of the Heart

"Guard your heart above all else, for it determines the course of your life."[81]

Last week I was preparing for the Children & Youth Sermon at our church. The scripture from Mark 7 centered on the Pharisees asking Jesus why his disciples didn't follow the tradition of washing their hands before eating. Jesus explained to them and others standing around that it was "not what goes into your body that defiles you; you are defiled by what comes from your heart."[82]

The Pharisees were more concerned about following the traditions of men and having clean hands than following God and having a clean heart.

I asked the group to think about what we do to keep our hearts clean. We clean our hands, but do we keep our hearts clean by protecting them from evil thoughts? Think about books we read, TV shows/movies we watch, and what we read on social media. Then listen to what language comes out of our mouths?

When we take the time to think about this, it becomes easier to grasp how we are bombarded just about every second of every day with information/stimulation of some sort. We hear, see, touch, feel, and eat what is coming into our bodies. All of these things are coming into our bodies and our minds and our hearts, but how do we guard against them remaining there? What if we let an evil thought

---

[81] Proverbs 4:23 (NLT).
[82] Mark 7:15-16 (NLT).

just sit for a little while? Before long, it would take root and begin to spread to our heart and minds. Doesn't the devil love this!!

How do we guard our hearts?

Protect Everything That Comes In - We need to use wisdom in what we allow into our hearts. What are we being influenced by? What are we listening to? What are we watching? Protect yourself from harm's way and a culture that is anti-God and replace it with things that are Godly. Your heart will then remain protected.

Cultivate An Atmosphere Of Community - There's no way to follow Jesus in isolation. Your heart needs people constantly pouring into you, and you need to be pouring into people. There's a constant flow coming in and out as you love and serve others.

Trust The Lord With Rest
We live in a culture that is so fast paced. While we run around like crazy, we often forget how negatively this affects our hearts. We are also telling God we don't trust Him in the process. When we rest in the Lord (including taking a full day off), we are declaring our dependency on Him. We are admitting we can't do life on our own.

Preach The Gospel To Yourself Each Day - The Gospel isn't just a "one time" thing and a ticket to heaven, but something we all need each and every day…every minute. The second we take our eyes off of the cross, we forget who we really are. Our hearts need to be reminded that while we still sin, we are forgiven, redeemed, and are children of God![83]

As you start your day with this truthful reminder, you'll have no choice but to glorify God in everything you do! Guard your hearts, my friends!

---

[83] Mike Mobley, "7 Ways to Guard Your Heart", www.beforethecross.com, accessed August 30, 2021, https://www.beforethecross.com/biblical-teachings/7-ways-to-guard-your-heart/.

Oh No! Did I Miss that Opportunity?

> Live wisely among those who are not believers, and
> make the most of every opportunity.[84]

Hasn't this fall shown us some of the most beautiful colors? A few weeks ago, I thought that the colors around here were not going to be as vivid and vivacious as in the past. I was sorely mistaken! My timing was all wrong!

On our weekly travels to South Boston, VA, I saw some beautiful plants along one section of the road – both yellow and deep red in color. Oh, how I wanted to stop and get some pictures, but there was always a reason I couldn't. In a week or so, those colors began to change and look less vivid and duller than when I first saw them. I was so saddened to have missed them because they were different from the foliage of the trees in this area. A missed opportunity! The same thing happened again along our South Boston route with another section of trees. Another missed opportunity!

Then I got frustrated with myself and began stopping whenever I saw a particularly beautiful tree. You wouldn't believe how many pictures I have on my phone! These colors in the past week have been outrageously beautiful! Very intense and dramatic!

Today I felt God's words in my spirit. He reminded me that when He gives us opportunities, it is up to us to seize them, or He can find someone else to give them to. Gulp! I swallowed hard on that one.

---

[84] Colossians 4:5 (NLT).

Using the trees as an example, He was showing me that when I didn't stop to get the pictures at the perfect time, I missed an opportunity which He had designated as the perfect time for me.

Now God gives us more opportunities than taking pictures of beautiful trees. They usually involve "being the presence of God" to others. Doing something in service for others – that kind word, a smile, a brief stop in their store to say "hello", a visit, walking them to their car to say "goodbye". It could also include having a conversation with another about what God has done for them, about God always being here and never leaving us, about God's track record of being with us through every difficult step forward and every pleasurable joy.

Next time you feel that God is showing you an opportunity to be in service for Him, I urge you to take it. Missed opportunities are just that – missed – and may not come around again.

God knows that you have what it takes to be that "presence of God' to others. Take it and do it! *No one else can do it exactly the way you can*, and that's why God wants you!

Oh, What A Relief It Is!

"'I see four men loose, walking in the midst
of the fire; and they are not hurt,
and the form of the fourth is like the Son of God.'"[85]

We have now entered the Fall of the year! A time for changing of leaf colors; cooler air; football season; s'mores over the fire pit; less grass to cut; new pumpkin-flavored drinks/muffins/cakes; AND a sigh of relief because we have passed the heat of the summer! It is not only the temperature heat but also the humidity which stifles us when we walk out of the doors of our homes on the summer mornings. Usually around the end of July/beginning of August, I have had it and stay inside as much as I can.

But then there is Fall! Today was the most beautiful day of all so far. The sky was a clear Carolina blue; the gentle breeze was blowing; the temperature was 75 degrees; the birds sounded louder and more joyous than usual; the squirrels were scampering around with nuts in their mouths; the air was crisper; the cirrus clouds were wispy and dancing across the sky; and you knew that God's creation had changed from summer to fall. What is astounding is to watch the larger birds as they ride the currents of the wind, just as a surfer rides the largest wave for as long as he/she can. It is beyond words to witness. It is beyond words to wonder how they feel as they exert

---

[85] Daniel 3:25 (NKJV).

their freedom in the skies just as we exert our freedom from the oppressing heat/humidity.

Mike and I completed our usual yard work – cut the grass, blew the sidewalks/driveway, edged the sidewalk/driveway. I hardly broke a sweat! (I am naturally cold-natured.) But then it happened. That God-thought came to me. The energy-depleting, draining heat and humidity of summer was over. The energy-depleting, draining heat from the enemy was over, and oh, what a relief it is!!

You know how it is when you have been battling for what seems like an eternity, and then the break-through comes. The relief washes over you from your head/mind to your feet. That burden is lifted. It is gone. What a relief it is! You and God have won this battle together!!

This is how I have felt this week after experiencing 90+ degree weather and heat indices of 100+ degrees. This cooler, beautiful weather has brought excitement, hope, joy to us – weary children of God – burdened by the heat, sticky and heavy schemes of the devil.

> "The thief does not come except to steal, and to kill, and to destroy."[86]

I am reminded of the story in Daniel 3 when Shadrach, Meshach, and Abed-Nego were thrown into the furnace for not worshipping the golden image of King Nebuchadnezzar. The King ordered the temperature of the furnace to be raised seven times hotter, and the three men were bound and thrown in.

> "Then he spoke, saying to his counselors, 'Did we not cast three men bound into the midst of the fire?' They answered and said to the king, 'True, O king.' 'Look!' he answered, 'I see four men loose, walking in the midst of the fire; and they are not hurt, and the form of the fourth is like the Son of God.'"[87]

---

[86] John 10:10 (NKJV).
[87] Daniel 3:24-25 (NKJV).

The "heat" in this story is like the heat from the enemy (and our summer). This trial has felt seven times hotter and more burdensome than previously. It has taken longer to fight through this battle and emerge victorious, but the Son of God has and will continue to be with us just as He was in the fire with the three Hebrew boys. He is the one fighting our battles with us. He is the one who has never left us and never will.

Therefore, we DO NOT GIVE UP!! And when that burden is lifted - as in the changing of the summer to fall — our hearts are overjoyed and soaring and absorbing all that God's creation has for us this season. We don't know how long this season will last — the physical or spiritual season — but praises to God that He will use it to help us, teach us, and strengthen us in His Son, Jesus!

We shout "Oh, What a Relief It Is!!!" Thank you, Jesus!

OPEN All The Time!

"My sheep listen to my voice; I know them, and they follow me."[88]

It was a GREAT morning to sleep with the rain coming down gently, but I finally decided that I needed to get up. After I prepared to get on the elliptical machine, I opened the bedroom door to get moving. All I heard was a loud noise which I couldn't decipher at first. Was it the AC kicking in? When I walked into the hallway, I looked toward the kitchen to see that the door was open. It was the rain I was hearing as it was coming down harder now. It was loud!

Mike had opened up the house because the temperature was lower outside than in the house. We love to have the windows and doors open whenever possible not only for the fresh air but also because of the sounds of nature.

Well, I certainly received a loud sound from the harder rain. It was like nothing I had heard in a long time. Either doors were closed previously, or the rain came during the night, but this definitely made an impact on me.

As I used the elliptical machine, the thought of the "loud rain" continued to swirl through my mind and spirit. I loved the sound, but I wouldn't have heard it to this degree if the doors had not been open. **OPEN**! That's the Word God gave me.

We hear sounds every day, all day. Sounds of nature; sounds

---

[88] John 10:27 (NLT).

of our environment; sounds of people talking. Are we "open" to hearing them or is it background noise to us? Are we receptive to these sounds and listening to them? Do they mean anything to us? The sounds of downtown Clarksville remind me of growing up here – the trucks traveling through town, horns honking, fire trucks rushing to answer a call, dogs barking, lawn mowers cutting, boats racing up and down the lake.

Do we hear the 15+ different kinds of birds chirping in our neighborhoods? Do we hear the car/truck sounds around town? Do we hear what people are saying to us? Maybe we do; maybe we don't.

I believe that God is asking if we are **OPEN** to hearing Him. Has He become background noise? Has His Word become boring? Has He not made himself known to us in dramatic ways like the shows on TV to get our attention?

God wants us to be **OPEN** to Him - through His Word, conversation with other Christians, hearing the Word of God preached/shared. If we are **OPEN** to Him, then we can absorb His Truth and produce good fruit just as the rains from today will produce good fruit.

Every drop of today's precious rain has soaked in. Don't you think God wants us to be **OPEN** to every precious Word so that every one of them can soak in to us?

> "The rain and snow come down from the heavens
>   and stay on the ground to water the earth.
> They cause the grain to grow,
>   producing seed for the farmer
>   and bread for the hungry.
> It is the same with my word.
>   I send it out, and it always produces fruit.
> It will accomplish all I want it to,
>   and it will prosper everywhere I send it."[89]

---

[89] Isaiah 55:10-11 (NLT).

Prayer:

May God grant us open eyes, open hearts and open ears that we may always hear when God speaks to us.

May God grant us discernment and wisdom to consistently recognize our Father's voice.

May God grant us willing hearts to obey God *quickly* when He gives us certain instructions.[90]

Let us all be OPEN and ready whenever and however God sends His Word to us!

---

[90] Bomi Jolly, "16 Encouraging Bible Verse about Hearing God's Word", www.jollynotes.com, accessed September 10, 2022, https://www.jollynotes.com/bible-verses/16-encouraging-bible-verses-about-hearing-gods-voice/.

Our God is More than a 3D Machine

"Search me, O God, and know my heart"[91]

Today was the day for my annual mammogram. I used to dread this and other preventive procedures, but I don't anymore because I realize they can only help me. This and other procedures like blood pressure checks, cholesterol checks, bone density tests, colonoscopy are meant to help us remain healthy and to stop a disease/condition in its tracks if it is found early.

So off I went. As I drove to the hospital, I prayed that God would assign an excellent technician to me and ensure that it was a smooth and easy process from beginning to end. Guess what! My check-in was simple and quick, which allowed me to arrive in the waiting room early. With less than a 5-minute wait, I was called. The technician seemed very good, and I was finished by 11:40 for an 11:30 appointment. Thank you, God!

On the way home, however, I thought about the procedure itself. The technician had me to stand in just the right position for the 3D machine - one arm up, head back out of the way, and my other arm behind my back. And you know, girls – HOLD YOUR BREATH! This 3D doesn't want anything in the way!

Then I began to ponder the 3D machine itself:

"This new 3D technology takes multiple images of each breast, allowing the radiologist to view the breast

---
[91] Psalm 139:23a (NLT).

layer-by-layer rather than viewing a single flat image. Fine details of the breast tissue were now visible and not hidden by the tissue immediately above or below."[92]

Think about this multi-million-dollar machine with its purpose to search for and detect any/all abnormal cells in the breast tissue. The 3D machine intently searches each layer of the breast, looking for what should not be there.

Is that what God does with us — intently searches us, looking at the aim or objective of our hearts and what should not be there?

> "For the word of God is alive and active. Sharper than any double-edged sword, it penetrates even to dividing soul and spirit, joints and marrow; it judges the thoughts and attitudes of the heart. Nothing in all creation is hidden from God's sight. Everything is uncovered and laid bare before the eyes of him to whom we must give account."[93]

His Word is so active and alive that it penetrates us completely, dividing our soul and spirit and joints and marrow into what is natural and what is spiritual. Nothing is hidden from God!

> "Search me, O God, and know my heart; test me and know my anxious thoughts. Point out anything in me that offends you, and lead me along the path of everlasting life."[94]

God, I am so glad you are not a machine, an idol, or a dead concrete image! You are alive and active and constantly searching us

---

[92] "The History of Mammography", www.ramsoft.com, published March 15, 2017, https://www.ramsoft.com/history-of-mammography/.
[93] Hebrews 4:12-13 (NIV).
[94] Psalm 139:23-24 (NLT).

and loving us. May we always believe and understand that your Word is what gives us life and not death. We thank you for all that we see and feel and touch here on this earth because we know that it all came from you! But most of all, we thank you that we have the faith to believe in the One whom we cannot see for His Word is truth!

Thank you for searching us and examining our hearts/our intents. Help us to rid ourselves of what is **not** like you!

> "The LORD does not look at the things people look at. People look at the outward appearance, but the LORD looks at the heart."[95]

No machine can or will ever be able to search us like God can!

---

[95] 1 Samuel 16:7b (NIV).

Remain Constant in the Treatment Plan

"For you created my inmost being;
you knit me together in my mother's womb.
I praise you because I am fearfully and wonderfully made;
your works are wonderful,
I know that full well."[96]

Recently, I have been experiencing pain in my left upper arm, especially when I move my arm laterally. Thankfully I am being seen by a very intuitive and experienced Physical Therapist in this area, and I know that I am on the road to recovery for this issue as well as others!

God tapped me in my brain midway through the initial assessment hour and said, "Pay attention." My senses were heightened at that point. This therapist had already given me valuable descriptions of what was happening in my shoulder area with the many muscles surrounding it, and now God was telling me to pay more attention for some reason.

While using a site on his smart phone that demonstrated visuals of how certain muscles functioned within the human body, my therapist described to me what was causing my discomfort. He showed me which muscles were being pulled away from their original positions causing them not to function for their originally intended purposes. It seems that something happened to cause a muscle to become

---

[96] Psalm 139:13-14 (NIV).

injured or not able to perform its main function. The surrounding muscles assist and compensate, thus enabling the injured person to complete a task. Those "helping" muscles try to perform their main functions as well as to help with the compromised muscles. But these "helping" muscles become overburdened while working extra hard with the sore muscles. It is like a chain reaction that eventually causes pain because something is not right.

Following our introduction, the therapist *expertly observed and listened to me* the entire time I was with him. He observed me walking to the assessment room, performing movements for him, and listened as I was answering his questions. He became aware of problem areas as he manipulated my shoulder and the various muscles surrounding it. He pinpointed every muscle, even the smallest ones, which needed help.

When he began manipulating those tight spots, which were quite painful but a good pain, then I became aware of my problem areas. I knew then that he knew what he was talking about! He had pinpointed the problem areas and had a treatment plan in mind. It would take several sessions to move the muscles back into their proper positions and strengthen them so that they would remain there where the therapist had re-located them. It would take time, and it would also take *consistency in implementing his treatment plan from that moment and into the future with consistency!*

Just as the therapist had taken certain steps to get me back on track physically, God expertly observed, listened, and then guided my faith journey through His perfect will to get me back on track spiritually. Look at what He showed me when He told me to "pay attention" to the therapist.

He was showing and telling me that this physical situation with my shoulder was like spiritual warfare – Satan's attacks. Just as a muscle can become weak, so our spirits can become weak. This spiritual weakness opens the door for the devil to tempt us. Right? We start to drift from the Godly path, or the "straight and narrow path", just like the injured muscle, but our Godly friends (the surrounding muscles) see this and reach out to help us. They attempt to bring us back to the right path. It may take a little nudge, or it may take extended time and effort for them, but it is always worth it to help another faithful friend.

Each muscle in our bodies has an assignment, or a task. Working together, they move our bodies in so many different ways. With the manipulation by the therapist, these muscles relaxed, strengthened, and moved into their right positions again. They returned to their original positions and performed their own important functions.

> "But our bodies have many parts, and God has put each part just where he wants it. How strange a body would be if it had only one part! Yes, there are many parts, but only one body. The eye can never say to the hand, "I don't need you." The head can't say to the feet, "I don't need you."
>
> In fact, some parts of the body that seem weakest and least important are actually the most necessary. And the parts we regard as less honorable are those we clothe with the greatest care. So we carefully protect those parts that should not be seen, while the more honorable parts do not require this special care. So God has put the body together such that extra honor and care are given to those parts that have less dignity. This makes for harmony among the members, so that all the members care for each other. If one part suffers, all the parts suffer with it, and if one part is honored, all the parts are glad.
>
> All of you together are Christ's body, and each of you is a part of it."[97]

We need the powerful intervention of the God who *expertly observes and listens* to us all the time! This is the God who already

---
[97] 1 Corinthians 12:18-27 (NLT).

knows us better than we know ourselves. He always knows what type of intervention or treatment plan we need – prayer, scripture, listening to praise music, a friend's prayer, etc. Over time, should we backslide, may we regain our strength and faith in order to start again upon that "straight and narrow path". Today and in the days to come, God desires that we use His strategies consistently and that we become/*remain committed to His "treatment plan" when/if we find ourselves in need of it*. This intervention from God along with the specific treatment plan we may need on our journey should keep us in the right position to become/remain connected to Him!

Rise and Shine!

"But we have this treasure in jars of clay to show that this all-surpassing power is from God and not from us. We are hard pressed on every side, but not crushed; perplexed, but not in despair; persecuted, but not abandoned; struck down, but not destroyed."[98]

Last summer the heat was scorching as well as dangerous! I looked over my plants and shrubs daily and tried to keep them watered and alive.

After lunch one day, as I was leaving the house, I decided to quickly check on my potted Gerber daisy plants. Much to my dismay, one of the blooms was drooping instead of standing up tall like it had been before. I examined it closely, but I couldn't figure out what had happened to it. I had a couple of appointments to get to, so I decided I would come back later to check on the bloom.

When I arrived home later that evening, guess what I saw? That Gerber daisy bloom was standing up tall and proud, showing off its God-given beauty just like nothing had ever been wrong. I gave it some water, along with a touch of Miracle Grow, and left it for the night.

The next day, much to my dismay, another drooping flower greeted me. I decided this was all related to the heat. That may have seemed like an obvious answer, but there had been some strange things happening to my plants that summer, so I wasn't necessarily expecting the obvious anymore!

---

[98] 2 Corinthians 4:7-9 (NIV).

I really felt sorry for this flower. It must have been tough being potted instead of growing in the true garden soil. It must have been tough sitting in a pot on a brick step with heat radiating all around instead of being planted directly in the cool ground. But this flower had continued to survive through daily watering and added nutrients.

God used unimpressive looking jars of clay to show that His power was not limited by a common container. Jars of clay were fragile and could easily break. These jars had many purposes in Jesus' time. They were exactly like the jars that contained my Gerber daisies. Even though the flowers drooped, they rose again after being nurtured with God's provisions.

God wants us to know that the power to survive is from Him and not from us or any human. How often does He use the weak, fragile, unimpressive people or objects to demonstrate His Word to us! We must learn to reach within ourselves to find His resources which will strengthen and nurture us. Then, like the flower on the Gerber daisy, we will be able to stand up tall, sharing those inner God-given gifts of love with one another!

Rise from the Pool

"Then Jesus said to him, 'Get up! Pick up your mat and walk.' At once the man was cured; he picked up his mat and walked."[99]

There is a familiar story in the Bible about Jesus healing the lame man at the Bethesda pool. Mike and I recently watched this story on an episode from "The Chosen", a fictional account of Jesus' life and ministry.

In "The Chosen" episode titled "The Perfect Opportunity"[100], Jesus and three of his disciples went to the pool at Bethesda to find "a man", as Jesus gave him no name. They found him laying on a mat near the pool, looking very haggard, feeble, and hopeless.

This story began by showing the man as a young boy when he fell out of a tree. His name was Jesse. He was paralyzed from the waist down and remained that way. He had laid beside the pool for 38 years, trying desperately to drag himself to the waters when they

---

[99] John 5:8-9 (NIV).
[100] Jenkins, Dallas, Dir, "The Perfect Opportunity", The Chosen, Season Two, Angel Studios, 2021, https://www.google.com/search?q=the+chosen+season+two+episode+four&client=avast-a-1&sxsrf=ALiCzsb4sArWC6PxPjgxAs07dSKnT3L3LA%3A1663171562298&ei=6vshY_fiEaqdwbkPzaah-A8&oq=The+Chosen+and+season+two&gs_lcp=Cgdnd3Mtd2l6EAEYATIGCAAQHhAWMgYIABAeEBYyBggAEB4QFjIGCAAQHhAWMgYIABAeEBYyBggAEB4QFjIGCAAQHhAWMgYIABAeEBYyBggAEB4QFjIGCAAQHhAWOgUIABCABABDoECCMQJzoFCAAQhgNKBAhBGABKBAhGGABQAFjbDmCfLmgAcAF4AIABkgGIAcwKkgEEMC4xMJgBAKABAcABAQ&sclient=gws-wiz.

began to bubble. The belief was that when the pool water began to bubble, it meant that an angel had stirred the water to produce healing powers to those who entered first.

But tried as he might, he could never make it in time. Others were pushing him aside, falling over him into the water as he crawled down the steps, and he was unable to reach the pool of "healing" water. Can you imagine doing this for 38 years?? But why not? He could not physically move his legs, and this was all that he had to focus on. He tried and tried and tried, but each time, he seemed to become more depressed.

Then Jesus came. Jesse did not know his name, but Jesus knew his and asked if he wanted to be healed? Jesse began to give one frustrating excuse after another of why he had not been able to reach the water and be healed yet. Jesus had not asked why he was not healed yet but if he wanted to be healed. Jesse cried, saying that it was all that he knew to do! He would have tried anything over these 38 years to heal his legs. Jesus knew that deep down, this man really didn't believe in the "healing" powers of this water, but it was the only hope that Jesse believed he had for his life.

Jesus told the man to look into his (Jesus') eyes – not at anyone else present. I believe it was then that the man was healed. Jesus told him to get up and take his mat with him. The man recognized "feeling" in his legs. He laughed, stood up, walked, jumped up and down. He was deliriously happy, and he hugged Jesus. Jesus then walked away smiling as the Pharisees were watching, because to carry a mat was considered work, and this was not allowed on the Sabbath. But that is another story!

As I pondered this, God impressed upon me the others who were laying around the pool waiting for their time to be healed by the stirred waters. They witnessed what happened to Jesse. They saw this man stand up and walk. What do you think they were thinking? How did they feel seeing "one of them" get up and walk away when the rest were left to wait for the next stirring of the waters? I don't know. There were so many others left at the pool who didn't know Jesus.

Why did Jesus go directly to this man? He knew that Jesse had faith from his upbringing. He knew that Jesse had lost hope and had hit "rock bottom". Has this ever happened to you or someone you know? Is this where you met Jesus – at rock bottom? Many of us have. It is a time of total surrender, and Jesus came to us at just the right time.

We don't know about the others around the pool. Many had come and gone since Jesse had been there during the 38 years. Were any "healed"? We don't have the answers to so many questions regarding stories recorded in the Bible.

Like those left waiting at the pool, we encounter people daily whose faith/beliefs we know nothing about. They may or may not be open to a test of faith. Not everyone will be ready to look Jesus in the eyes and "rise from their pool."

Jesse looked into Jesus' eyes and KNEW he was healed. It was Jesse's faith which was rekindled when he looked into Jesus' eyes and the hope for his life rose up in him. Jesse's faith allowed him to rise from the pool.

Don't be afraid to look Jesus in His eyes. Rise from the pool! He will not let you rise alone!

That Simple Touch

"For where two or three are gathered together in My name, I am there in the midst of them."[101]

After returning home from the virus-impacted wedding in DE, I continuously relived many special moments from the weekend.

Chris, Lis and her parents planned an immediate-family-only wedding that would be filled with both elegance and simplicity - not what Lis had dreamed of but still so sweet and intimate.

Our new daughter, Lis (Forget DIL! She's a daughter!), missed the bridesmaids who could not attend due to their location and the virus. There were distant family and very close friends who could not attend, but that never stopped the incredible planning for this Disney-loving young woman who married the man of her dreams - our son, Chris.

On Thursday night, there was a gathering for the girls only. Friday morning was dropping Bear (our son's dog) at the groomer and then going to get our mani-pedis. Friday night was the rehearsal dinner with words from Mike and me as well as Lis's parents. Then it was Saturday! Saturday was THE day for make-up, hair, and seeing the bride for the first time in THE dress. Oh my! Yes, tears came.

We were at Lis's sister-in-law's house for Saturday morning but then drove to her parents' home for the wedding (five-minute walk through the woods, but we rode on Gators and golf carts). The men

---

[101] Matthew 18:20 (NKJV).

were upstairs, and the women were downstairs. Upstairs, some of the men left the room after their toasts, and all who remained were Chris, Mike, and Lis's Dad, Kevin. Mike and Kevin knew this time was just for the three of them, so they prayed over Chris, so sweet and powerful!

Meanwhile downstairs, the women gathered around Lis as she sat in her chair – each woman with a hand on her and offering a prayer for Chris and her. During the prayers, I felt Lis's simple touch as she reached for my hand, which was laying on her shoulder. This simple touch was the most precious touch of the entire weekend. It was a beautiful ceremony, and yes, Bear was part of it. He was there wearing a sign which read "My 2 humans are getting married today."

Since we have returned home, my thoughts have been filled with memories from the weekend, but the one which comes up every time is that of Lis's simple touch on my hand while we were praying. Today I thought of Jesus and what His simple touch meant to so many. They were touches of healing; touches of compassion; touches of learning who God the Father really is; and touches of serving, which is what Jesus came to earth to do – to serve and give God the glory as He taught about His Father.

During the pandemic, it has been, and still is, so difficult not being able to touch others with a hug, a handshake, or a pat on the back. A simple touch can mean so much to others and even more when given by Jesus. Let us not forget to continue to pray for others, call others, and talk to others. We are certainly learning not to take these things for granted. Let us also remember: With God's help, we will get through this.

The 5-Fold Ministry

*"And He Himself gave some to be apostles,
some prophets, some evangelists,
and some pastors and teachers"*[102]

Recently Mike and I went hiking at the state park across the lake from our town. It was a beautiful Saturday morning which was already beginning to heat up, but thankfully we were under the cooling canopy of the trees. As we walked along, we noticed many parts of God's creation - so many different trees (newer, tender ones and older, stronger ones), ferns, weeds, flowers. The birds were singing and calling to each other. It was my kind of day!

But near the end of the trail, I happened to look at, or God turned my eyes toward, a group of trees. There were 5 trees about 10 inches in diameter forming a semi-circle, and a young sapling positioned at the head of the semi-circle. Yes, it was a God moment, and God told me that this was the 5-fold ministry surrounding one of his newest disciples. It looked as if the trees were teaching, protecting this disciple and mentoring it. Wow!

> *"And He Himself gave some to be apostles, some prophets, some evangelists, and some pastors and teachers, for the equipping of the saints for the work of ministry, for the edifying of the body of Christ, till we all come to the unity of the faith and of the*

---

[102] Ephesians 4:11 (NKJV).

knowledge of the Son of God, to a perfect man, to the measure of the stature of the fullness of Christ."[103]

Verse 11: Isn't it just like God to surround us with those who can mentor us and teach us about His Word and take us deeper into the meaning of his truth – the real truths of the scriptures? We each have different learning styles, but God assures us that He will send those who can teach us in just the right way for the "style" God gave us.

Verses 12-13: Tells us why God did this. The work of these mentors will be for the "equipping of the saints for the work of ministry, for the edifying of the body of Christ".

WHICH WILL RESULT IN: bringing all of us into the "unity of the faith." Building and uniting the body of Christ into one unit!

> *"There is* one body and one Spirit, just as you were called in one hope of your calling; one Lord, one faith, one baptism; one God and Father of all, who *is* above all, and through all, and in you all."[104]

Our God is a giving God because he gave us the ones to teach us and mentor us. Now we must continue to learn so we can grow and teach others. Praise God!!

---

[103] Ephesians 4:11-13 (NKJV).
[104] Ephesians 4:4-6 (NKJV).

The Babe That Melts our Hearts

"God blessed them and said to them, 'Be
fruitful and increase in number;
fill the earth and subdue it.'"[105]

What is it about a baby that makes us melt into a doting grandparent, uncle/aunt, cousin, best friend?? Remember the first time we held that newborn? Our heart was stolen without us even realizing it! And then we began that "baby talk". Where does that come from?? It just seems to happen automatically – look into the eyes of the infant; open mouth; out comes baby talk!

Even before becoming a grandparent, I have experienced this with others' newborns. It simply amazes me that these changes occur without me having to consciously think about it!

During Advent, I thought about the baby whom God sent to us. Yes, the baby Jesus. Do you think he heard that "baby talk" as well? Probably so.

Do you think that the baby Jesus impacted his parents and family with his cuteness? Do you think their hearts melted when he cooed, laughed, and blew bubbles? Yes, I do.

Research has shown that a baby's cuteness is "designed to appeal

---

[105] Genesis 1:28a (NIV).

to all our senses to trigger our care-giving behaviors, which are vital for them to survive and thrive."[106]

This suggests that babies do and can affect us by their cuteness – their smiles, coos, smells, eyes. There must be an effect so that our natural care-giving nature will move into high-gear to take care of them and help them to not only survive but to thrive!

Can babies bring healing and hope to family members? I believe that babies can definitely make an impact on various family situations as God uses them. Just as Jesus drew people to Him as the Son of God, babies seem to draw people also. There is a renewed sense of hope and wonder and adventure, and "there is so much out there for you, little one". We all see these little ones with a future that is wide open to them. We want so much for these babes, and we want to give them more than we had – a better chance in life, an education, a job they are passionate about, a love of sports/writing/music/dance, travel. This list is endless.

All babies were created in God's image. God's breath is in them. It is up to us as mothers, fathers, grandparents, uncles/aunts, cousins, best friends to nurture these children, teach them about this God who created them and give them the best of ourselves.

"Children live what they learn."[107] May they learn about Jesus and to be kind and loving to one another.

---

[106] IANS, "Why Babies Melt Our Hearts", The Indian Express, June 7, 2016, https://indianexpress.com/article/lifestyle/life-style/why-babies-are-cute-2839827/

[107] Nolte, Dorothy Law, "Children Live What They Learn", www.Childrenlearnwhattheylive.com, Workman Publishing Co., 1955, https://childrenlearnwhattheylive.com/.

The Beauty of His Holiness

"Give unto the Lord the glory due to His name: worship the Lord in the beauty of Holiness."[108]

This morning my reading was from *Jesus Calling*, and this captured my entire being:

> "I created beauty to declare the existence of My holy Being. A magnificent rose, a hauntingly glorious sunset, oceanic splendor — all these things were meant to proclaim My Presence in the world.
>
> How precious are My children who are awed by nature's beauty; this opens them up to my holy Presence. Even before you knew Me personally, you responded to My creation with wonder. This is a gift, and it carries responsibility with it. Declare My glorious Being to the world."[109]

How many times have you said or heard someone say, "Look at that sunrise/sunset! How can anyone see that and not believe there is a God!" You have just declared His glorious Being, the beauty of His Holiness with those words.

As each day goes by, be intentional about seeing His beauty

---

[108] Psalm 29:2 (NKJV).
[109] Sarah Young, *Jesus Calling*, (Tennessee, Thomas Nelson, 2011) 221.

and seeing Him. Even if there are no flowers blooming, there are hummingbirds and other birds. There are such a variety of green leaves on the trees, and when there are no leaves on the limbs, take a look at how the tree is shaped and its unique limbs with buds preparing for the next spring. The sky is constantly changing when different types of clouds move through the atmosphere. The stars are a glorious wonder when we try to imagine how many there are. What are the tree shadows showing you or the shadows on the lake as clouds pass overhead? In the mornings, I see the dew drops on the bottom of the white fence next to our yard and what a thing of beauty they are.

From time to time, I share pictures with you and declare the Beauty of His Holiness. I pray that you see His Beauty outside your window throughout the year. Share it with others so that they too will be intentional about not only seeing God's beauty but seeing God and knowing that He does exist. Look beyond the window and inside your heart!

The Deafening Silence of No Electrical Power!!

"All things were made through Him, and without Him nothing was made that was made."[110]

What a winter and what a God! Today I write about the almost quietness of the outside and inside world due to the ice storm which came last night. I say "almost" because we have no power but do have the generator running to keep the fridge and freezer operating as well as a light and our phone-charging station.

With no power, there is no internet; no TV; no lights; no music; no online puzzles to mesh together. This quiet time has been different. Lord, what do you want me to do? What are you trying to "show" me?

While sitting in silence in front of the gas logs, I looked around at every little thing in our family room, outside the windows, and even through my senses of touch, hearing, seeing, etc. There is nothing that He did not make! God has created so many people with skills to help mankind, and here we are today with a variety of modern conveniences. You may say that God didn't create the web or drive-alone cars or Zoom services, but He did! Through the people He has created over time, He has given them knowledge and wisdom and curiosity and adventure to take us where we have not been before. It makes you wonder what is yet to come!

---

[110] John 1:3 (NKJV).

Then there are those who have gifts from God but either choose not to use them or to use them in sinful ways. We have a choice to use those gifts or not, and we have a choice to submit to God's will or not. He does not force us to do it. It is up to us to surrender our lives to Him and the plans He has for us. Some may view "surrender" in negative terms but not when God is involved!

> "*Surrender* is a battle term. It implies giving up all rights to the conqueror. When an opposing army surrenders, they lay down their arms, and the winners take control from then on. Surrendering to God works the same way. God has a plan for our lives and surrendering to Him means we set aside our own plans and eagerly seek His. The good news is that God's plan for us is always in our best interest (Jeremiah 29:11), unlike our own plans that often lead to destruction (Proverbs 14:12). Our Lord is a wise and beneficent victor; He conquers us to bless us."[111]

God, I thank you for this silence, this stillness, this darkness and the dancing shadows of the gas logs. You have given me an experience that happens so infrequently in today's world. An experience with no distractions and the time to focus on you.

It has been an experience which has emphasized your power, your creation, your compassion for us. Just as you supplied everything for Adam and Eve in the Garden of Eden, you have supplied everything we could ever ask for in today's world. It takes a deafening silence of no electrical power to realize this and to thank you and praise you for all that you have provided for us.

---

[111] "What Does It Mean To Surrender To God?", https://www.gotquestions.org/surrender-to-God.html, updated January 4, 2020.

The Deception of the Enemy

"My son, pay attention to what I say;
turn your ear to my words.
²¹ Do not let them out of your sight,
keep them within your heart;
²² for they are life to those who find them
and health to one's whole body."[112]

We recently had the first snowfall of the year. When I went outside and looked on the black tarp laying on the ground next to our driveway, I realized that it looked like a topographical map of some mountain ranges. Wow! It reminded me of the view while flying out to California a few years ago. Thank you, God, for showing this to me!

But as I looked at the tarp, I realized that if I had zoomed in with my camera to take a close-up picture and put it on social media, those seeing it would have thought it was an actual topographical map. They would have been deceived!

We can so easily be deceived by the world and by others. When we look at others, we do not see what is going on inside of them - physically, mentally, emotionally, or spiritually. Sometimes people will show their feelings "on their sleeve", but many times, someone will say that they are "doing fine" when, in reality, they are crying

---

[112] Proverbs 4:20-22 (NIV).

inside or are in physical pain. We are deceived, although not in a mean-spirited way.

Our enemy is the greatest deceiver of all time. His cunning approach to each of us will hit us right where it hurts the most. He can tell us to put on a happy face and not let others know how we feel. We become the deceivers because of his influence in our minds. Remember the Garden of Eden? Talk about deception!

What are we to do? How do we handle this deception from the enemy? How do we handle this deception toward our friends? We handle it the only way that is right, and that is to take it to God. Talking to our closest friends usually gives us some relief, but God is the long-term/everlasting listener, problem solver and healer. We need to call on the name of Jesus right then and there.

He already knows what we are going through. Not only that, but He also knows the depths of that with which we are suffering/struggling. We are engrained in His heart and in His mind. He has called us by name. He sees the inside as well as the outside. A picture may be worth a thousand words, but God can describe us perfectly because He created us and doesn't need a picture.

Be careful when listening to someone who tells you that they are fine. I pray they are, and I respect their privacy if they prefer not to talk about it. Just know that they may be hurting inside. We can pray! If someone asks for prayer, pray for them at that moment. If they suggest not to pray in a public place, you can pray silently or walk to another, more private location. God hears!

This is a fallen world, and many people are hurting. Therefore it is so important to actively pray for that person(s) In Jesus' Name. He has given us the authority to loose what is in heaven (His healing) here on earth, and we state it in *His* name. It is through His power and not ours that others are healed, and strongholds are broken.

It is also important to be part of the body of Christ; to be in communion with each other; to help each other through our tiresome and most difficult days; to read our Bibles daily; and to praise God in the triumphs of our fulfilling days.

Pray *In Jesus' Name!*

The First Step - A Risk or the Real Thing

"Show me your ways, Lord, teach me your paths.
⁵ Guide me in your truth and teach me,
for you are God my Savior, and my hope is in you all day long."[113]

One of the volunteer opportunities which I really enjoy is assisting others with playing Bingo at the local nursing home. Believe me when I say that Bingo is serious business there!! They do not want to miss it, nor do they want people to delay the game once we get started!!

Have you ever played Bingo? It is much like buying a lottery ticket or a raffle ticket. You play the "game" by taking a chance; a risk; a shot in the dark. You don't have a magic formula for ensuring that you "win". There is nothing you can wear or chant which will improve your chances. Your odds of winning certainly decrease as the number of people playing these games increases.

So why do we participate in these risky ventures? Why are we so obsessed with this? Even as I am helping these residents, I can see their disappointment when they don't win! And the prizes are snacks or a small stuffed animal, which are highly treasured! In the community when the prize is money, I can easily understand the attraction. Who wouldn't want to win some of these larger monetary prizes? Usually, you must pay to play, right? So, if you don't win big, then you are losing money. I ask again - why do we do this?

---

[113] Psalm 25:4-5 (NIV).

Is it the thrill and excitement of winning? Is it a mark of achievement? Is it that competitive nature in us? I am sure the reasons are as varied as the people who play – "it's my recreation"; "my friend won big last week so I'm going to try"; "it's my birthday and I'm celebrating"; "I'm a risk-taker and this is fun"; "I like the challenge"; "it's what I do every Tuesday".

Then let me ask you this. Have you ever given your life to Christ or led someone in that way? Was that risky? Was it like taking a chance on something that you weren't sure about nor had control over? Did it feel like a "shot in the dark"? I have read stories about people who were hanging from their last thread and decided to give God a try since nothing else had worked. They were awfully glad they did. Others may have taken this step because a friend had done so. Some may have felt that "tugging" in their spirit but didn't realize what it was and decided to move forward toward Christ. Again, the reasons are as varied as the people who have given their life to Christ.

However, the key is in the act of taking that first step. You have to first take that step toward either 1) a life of risk and chance or 2) a life of love and dependence on God, who is a sure thing and constant presence in our lives.

1. Once you take the step to buy a lottery ticket or buy a raffle ticket or play Bingo, you have lost control, but who have you lost it to? Who controls the selection of the winning ticket or the numbers called in Bingo? A machine; a computer; something programmed by man to randomly select the "winning" combination, or someone turning the wheel for Bingo numbers.
2. Once you take the step to give your life to Christ, you have lost control here as well, but who have you lost it to? Who controls the acceptance (not "selection" because He receives all who come to Him) of the newest saved soul? It is not a machine or a computer or something programmed by man. It is our Almighty Creator God! He has you now as one of His own because He called you "before the foundations of the

world."[114] He will continue to love you, nurture you, teach you by the Holy Spirit, encourage you, send others to you to help along the way. He will never leave you nor forsake you. *It is a sure thing! Why wouldn't we choose this step forward?*

When it comes to God, I don't believe that there is any risk being taken to follow Him because I know He's got my back! You can count on Him and not wonder if He'll show up or answer; you can depend on His everlasting love which has never changed; you can experience life to the fullest through Him. What more do you want? When you compare a game of chance with a life of assuredness, I'll go with the sure thing every day.

Cut your losses from the past! Go with the sure thing. Take that first step and go with Who you can count on, Who loves you more than anything, and Who you know you can trust!

---

[114] Ephesians 1:4 (NIV).

Standing Alone can be Tough

"If you keep quiet at a time like this, deliverance and relief for the Jews will arise from some other place, but you and your relatives will die. Who knows if perhaps you were made queen for just such a time as this?"[115]

This year, I didn't plant any flowers next to our side porch because we were having our porch renovated into a sunroom. I had covered the ground with black plastic to kill any weeds that tried to show themselves during renovation.

It was such a loooong summer without flowers! While Mom lived here, she planted gerber daisies beside the porch for years, and I have done the same since living here with the addition of zinnias last year. That area now looks pretty bare with black plastic over it.

Guess what God did??!! He surprised me with one zinnia plant growing right next to the brick foundation of the porch. A few weeks ago, I used my "plant identifier" app on my phone to verify that it was indeed a zinnia. Yup! It has been exciting to watch it grow, and last week I had to stake it because it was leaning so much toward the sun and falling over!

My heart was blessed by this one plant. It actually reminded me of how often we have to stand alone, meaning physically separating ourselves or intellectually separating ourselves. There can be a variety

---

[115] Esther 4:14 (NLT).

of reasons, such as not having the same belief(s) as others, not agreeing with issues raised by others, or not being seen as supportive of a cause that others support.

It has not been easy for me to stand alone at times. I have always been a "people pleaser" and have gone along with the crowd many times. Sometimes I have followed the crowd and later really thought about what I did and changed my mind on that issue. Growing up has been tough!

Have you ever been tested in your faith? I remember years ago in Durham when a friend of my sons tried to commit suicide but, thankfully, was unsuccessful. Mike, myself, and the boys went to the hospital to gather with friends from the youth group and other church members. I remember distinctly listening to one of the youth leaders talking about how awful the situation was, and there was little hope that he would survive and/or survive with his faculties intact. God's spirit rose up in me like never before. I don't remember all that I said, but I did talk to her about the power of God; the hope of God; and the healing of God. Don't claim death when God is in the picture!! Thankfully, he did survive and is a healthy young man.

There have been other times when I have felt alone due to my convictions/faith beliefs based on my life experiences, but how will we know if we were made for "such a time as this" unless we speak up? Some people have been very comfortable with speaking up, but it has been hard for me unless God really moved me.

Sometimes "standing alone" means physically standing alone. But God has a way of drawing some to us who are like-minded. He has done this more since we moved to Clarksville than before. Is it Clarksville? Well, it is a great little town on the lake, but it is the Spirit of those with whom God has connected me. I pray for that connection to continue to grow!

Each day of the season, I examined my zinnia. It was a beautiful pink. I continued to see more buds!! By the end of summer, this zinnia flower was no longer standing alone because it had new blooms coming to join in the celebration! Praise God for knowing just what I needed and when I needed it to keep me standing!

The Gift that Keeps on Giving

"...And be sure of this: I am with you always, even to the end of the age".[116]

Here we are with less than 2 weeks until Christmas!! How is your stress level? Are you prepared with presents for all on your list and the meal planning that has to be done? I'm sure that the last thing you need right now is not having a gift for that special friend/family member who means so much to you. I have a recommendation for the "gift that keeps on giving"!

For as long as I can remember, my mom wanted to give gifts to special people which would last, or in other words, they would "keep on giving". I'm talking about items such as cross-stitch sayings/quilts, wooden items which Dad had made, meaningful books, or family heirlooms. Whenever we made suggestions of clothing or electronics which mom could give us kids, she wouldn't have anything to do with that! She always ended up finding the perfect gift for each of us.

As "perfect" and meaningful as these gifts were, they were limited in how much they could "give" to us. Naturally every time we have looked at or used them, the fond memories have returned to us from times past. How grateful I am for those memories from each and every item!

However, I am here to tell you about a different kind of gift that will keep on giving for the rest of your life!

---

[116] Matthew 28:20 (NLT).

It is all about a man named Jesus. If you don't know Him, it is time that you did. You may meet Him at the coffee shop, at a women's meeting, at a dinner with friends, at a ball game, through an intimate conversation with a Godly friend. The settings are endless, but the people who share Jesus with you are priceless. You may meet Him for the 1st time and begin a relationship with Him, OR you may already know Him but want to know Him in a deeper way. Regardless of the circumstances, your relationship with Him will be a gift that will keep on giving – everyday!!

He is not an inanimate object but a living, divine spirit dwelling within you once you accept Him as your Savior. He is the one whose death on the cross defeated death and sin. It allows us to have the benefits of a personal and divine relationship with God and Jesus through the Holy Spirit. And we gain the gift of eternal life! Whenever we need Him, He is here. It doesn't matter where we are, He is always with us providing for our every need. We can talk to Him 24/7, but we must believe and have faith in Him.

Whenever you need a gift for someone, consider giving the gift that keeps on giving every day. It is a different kind of gift because it is eternal. Whenever you or someone else experiences Jesus, you will have an encounter that you won't soon forget. It will be the greatest gift ever given and received!

The Golden Rule - It's About What We Give

"Do to others as you would like them to do to you."[117]

What if I came up to you and pushed you?
What if I just called you a bad name?

Then again, what if I came up to you and told you how much I liked you? Would that be better? What would you do or say if I thanked you for standing up for me or gave you some other compliment?

When people do bad things to us, like pushing us or calling us a name, it makes us want to do bad things back to them. But when people do or say nice things to us, we want to do or say nice things to them.

Jesus said that we're supposed to be nice to everyone, even if they're mean to us.

> "But to you who are listening I say: Love your enemies, do good to those who hate you, bless those who curse you, pray for those who mistreat you."[118]

That means that we should treat everyone, even the mean people,

---

[117] Luke 6:31 (NLT).
[118] Luke 6:27-29 (NIV).

the way we want to be treated. We do it regardless of how they treat us.

But how do we get beyond our natural reactions? We must look past what they did and toward Christ.

Our natural tendency is to get even or avoid those people who hurt us. God is calling each of us to keep on blessing them even when they hurt us. It can be really tough, but then again, it's not always easy being a Christian.

But here is something that may help you. Think about this:

<u>It's quite possible that when we show love, it will transform the lives of others</u>. You see, we may never know what the other person's story is unless they tell us. Maybe they just had a death in their family; they are not loved where they live; they are bullied by others. There are 2 sides to every story, and we don't always know what the other person is going through.

Our love may help them to see things in a different way.

Living by the Golden Rule is not about what we *get*. It's about what we *give*. We must not look at the hurt but look toward Christ.[119]

---

[119] Rev. Stephen R. Wilson, *Lesson: The Golden Rule*, www.ministry-to-children.com, updated June 1, 2020, https://ministry-to-children.com/lesson-the-golden-rule/.

The Protection of a Leaf

"He who dwells in the secret place of the Most High
Shall abide under the shadow of the Almighty.
He shall cover you with His feathers,
And under His wings you shall take refuge;
His truth *shall be your* shield and buckler."[120]

I love the spring time of year when the silver maple tree is changing by the day. The buds are expanding into pretty, little leaves which are growing larger each day. Creation is unfolding before my eyes!

When I was on the elliptical this morning, God brought my attention to these newly expanding leaves – from bud to a minuscule unfolding of each leaf to a small but recognizable green maple leaf. He also showed me how the leaves at the end of each branch were larger than those under them. They were at different stages of growth, but the ones at the branches' ends were the largest. They actually provided a covering, like feathers or wings, for the smaller ones underneath.

You all know by now that I am a very visual person. When God placed this message in my spirit, I knew that the larger leaves reminded me of Psalm 91, with the "feathers" or "wings" protecting those underneath. The smaller buds/leaves are like us when we are feeling fearful, uncertain, doubtful of all that is happening around us. Sometimes we have misplaced our strong faith for our

---

[120] Psalm 91:1, 4 (NKJV).

"not-as-strong" faith and have taken our eyes from Jesus. "Not-as-strong" faith can only take us but so far in life. The more life we experience, the stronger our faith is required to become. If not, we just won't survive very well.

We must stay under the "shadow of the Almighty", just like the smaller, not as strong and easily swayed, leaves. Our faith must become stronger as we grow, experience life, pray, and read God's Word. These smaller leaves have thrived and grown under the shadow of the larger ones.

The larger leaves symbolize those who are experienced with life and provide shelter and guidance for us. They protect us, teach us, love us, and show us the way to God. Soon it will be our turn as the larger leaves to protect, teach, love, and show others the way to God.

May we strengthen our faith and trust in God throughout these current times and keep our eyes upon Jesus! May God bless each of you immeasurably as we move forward each day in the "shadow of the Almighty"!

There Was Jesus

> "And we know that all things work together
> for good to those who love God,
> to those who are the called according to *His* purpose."[121]

As I think back over the summer - the time in which God told me to WAIT - I see there was Jesus with me the entire time. Yes, even when I didn't realize it or think about it, He was there!

Do you know how it feels when you take a look back? It's as if your spiritual eyes can see what your natural eyes could not see before, and it all makes sense now. That sweet moment of marriage in June 2020 for our younger son, Chris, and his best friend, Elisabeth; the tenderness of having family-only, including his dog, Bear; the mother-son dance where he twirled me around; the words of the pastor spoken over them as God blessed their marriage. There was Jesus!

Then there was the message of waiting which God spoke to me in July - waiting on Him, His direction, and His timing on several issues. I prayed, listened, and observed. There was Jesus!

Then our church went back to in-person worship in August 2020. Even with adhering to the required restrictions, it was such a joy to see those fellow members of Centenary! We were finally together again in the sanctuary, even though we were spaced apart. There was Jesus!

---

[121] Romans 8:28 (NKJV).

Recently there have been disappointments, and the waiting has become more difficult. My patience and focus on God have been stretched. Still there was Jesus!

God brought someone to me to say a word or text a message that was right on time! He sent a friend to help me see the wrongly timed email I was about to send. There were the lonely times when I wondered where everyone went (or so the enemy wanted me to think!), and I talked with God about it. He knew what I needed, and the next day, one of Mom's friends called to check on me at just the right time. There was Jesus!

Recently Mike and I traveled to Delaware for Elisabeth's 4th-time-rescheduled Bridal Shower, and I realized on Friday night at 9 pm that I had not brought my clothes for the shower! Go ahead and laugh in disbelief because I sure did! What a sinking feeling that was, but I texted Elisabeth to tell her and apologize. You know what she texted back? She said not to worry. She would pick out several dresses for me to try on since we wear about the same size, and while she was getting her make-up done the next morning, I could try them and find one to wear. Thankfully we are very close in height! WOW! On Saturday morning, I tried on dresses and sure enough, there was one I could wear! Saved by my DIL!!! And there was Jesus!

During each of these examples, someone could say that I was "lucky" for these things to happen to support me, help me in the waiting, and bless me. Take a look at the definitions of "luck" - a "state of happening by chance; something good which happens by chance".[122] The word "chance" means "something that happens unpredictably without discernible human intention or observable cause".[123] When something is unpredictable, it does not guarantee anything good to happen. When God is in the picture, He works all things together for good for those who love Him.

My friends, I do not believe in "luck". I want to believe in something that is sure; that is solid; that is true; that is constant; about

---

[122] *The Free Dictionary*, "Luck", https://www.thefreedictionary.com/lucky.
[123] *Merriam-Webster Dictionary*, "Chance", https://www.merriam-webster.com/dictionary/chance.

which there is NO DOUBT! *And there was Jesus!* He is the one who is sure; who is solid; who is true; and who is constant. He is not an object. He is the Son of God who paid the ransom for our very lives.

Jesus has been here for me every minute of every hour. Has He been there for you? This summer was a time of waiting and learning what God wanted me to learn. It seems as if He has been teaching me more and more as each season comes. I share it with you in hopes that it will have meaning for you and others who read this.

Trusting Without Borders

"Those who know your name trust in you, for you, Lord, have never forsaken those who seek you."[124]

As I listened to the song "Oceans" by Hillsong United, I was overwhelmed by the depth of trust described in these words.

> "Spirit lead me where *my trust is without borders*
> Let me walk upon the waters, wherever You would call me
> Take me *deeper than my feet could ever wander*
> And my *faith will be made stronger, in the presence of my Savior*"[125] (emphasis mine)

Do you feel like your trust in God is so deep that it is "without borders"? Merriam-Webster Dictionary defined "border" as "an outer part or edge, the outer edge of something."[126] If we think about the phrase "without borders", it means simply that – something that has no limits or constraints or an outer boundary. That is absolute trust - no doubt about anything whatsoever!

My trust in God has grown deeper over the years, but I cannot

---

[124] Psalm 9:10 (NIV).
[125] Hillsong United, "Oceans", 2nd song on *Zion*, Michael Guy Chislett production, 2013.
[126] *Merriam-Webster Dictionary*, "Borders", https://www.merriam-webster.com/dictionary/borders.

say that it is at a level of "without borders". Sometimes there are situations in which I find myself feeling anxious. Maybe I don't know what to expect under the circumstances or maybe I am being questioned about something that I am not prepared for. But instead of trusting God to lead me through or to give me the appropriate words to say, I am more focused on my fleshly symptoms of anxiousness. I am not trusting God "without borders"!

What happens if we don't totally trust God? Let me share one thought.

Take a look at the word "trust". Spell it out - **T.R.U.S.T**. If you remove the "T", you are left with "**RUST**". Let me tell you about rust:

> - As a noun, it means "the reddish brittle coating formed on iron especially when chemically attacked by moist air and composed essentially of hydrated ferric oxide; corrosive or injurious influence or effect"
> - As a verb, it means to "degenerate especially from inaction, lack of use, or passage of time"[127]

Do you understand what will happen if we are not trusting God to lead us? We will begin to **RUST**! We will be attacked by the enemy; a corrosive coating will begin to form in us. We will degenerate from inaction. We will become corroded from lack of use of the power that God gave us.

For repairing rust spots, general recommendations included frequent cleaning and waxing and the application of various *oils*. How about our own "rust" spots? Don't they need to be cleansed with *God's Word and anointed with oil*?

At the first sign of rust, we can prevent further damage by attending to problem spots immediately. It is important to react quickly because light rust damage could indicate a higher level of unseen deterioration. It's what is unseen, or in the darkness, that

---

[127] *Merriam-Webster Dictionary*, "Rust", https://www.merriam-webster.com/dictionary/rust.

will affect our trust in God. We must have faith and remain in His marvelous light and trust in His Word.

We must be diligent to stay in the Word so that the distractions in our lives don't confuse us and begin the rusting or degenerating process. God's Word is our anointing, and nothing can penetrate it as long as we remain covered by it. It is the anointing that destroys the yoke or the degeneration of our faith. We are covered in His robe of righteousness, and we can't afford to lose or destroy that covering!

Trusting and believing in God are critical to the faith of Christians. But trusting "without borders" must be the ultimate trust in God. I pray that we all will get there!

Letter to Santa

"'For I know the plans I have for you,' declares the
Lord, 'plans to prosper you and not to harm you,
plans to give you hope and a future.'"[128]

I love seeing our youngest children at church, and today was no exception. After the service, one of our 4-year-olds came out of the Children's church room and handed me a red paper. Glued to it was a cut out letter to Santa. It was a "fill-in-the-blank" letter stating what a child would want for Christmas.

When she gave it to me, she said that it was for Christmas; it was a letter to Santa. I questioned her about whether or not she really wanted me to have it. Very determinedly, she said "yes, put it in the mail to Santa"! Without hesitation, I agreed to do so!

We are currently 7 months away from Christmas, but she is already planning ahead. Santa certainly has her attention. She knows how important he is and that she will get some presents from him!

Maybe we should all take a lesson from her and be sure that we have planned ahead for our future and where we will be spending it. Because you know why? God has some presents to give to us, too, and these "presents", or His presence, will be with us forever!

So get your letter in the mail, or better yet, talk to Him today!!

---

[128] Jeremiah 29:11 (NIV).

Upholstered by God

"Search me, O God, and know my heart;
test me and know my anxious thoughts.
Point out anything in me that offends you,
and lead me along the path of everlasting life."[129]

We were returning home from a vacation in Nags Head, NC and drove through Plymouth, NC. This was a small town with the typical food/restaurant signs and billboards on the sides of the road advertising what they had to offer to travelers.

I happened to get a quick glance at a couple of signs attached to a tall post. At the top, the sign read "Jesus is Coming". Below it was another sign which I didn't have time to read because I was looking at the bottom sign which advertised a local upholstery company. I laughed as I read to Mike what the signs showed. Jesus is Coming and Get your furniture upholstered!

However, it wasn't until a couple of minutes later that I realized what God was saying to me through the signs. Jesus is coming. He can upholster or reupholster anyone!

Have you ever had a piece of furniture upholstered or re-covered? My mother had 2 wingback chairs in our formal living room which she had re-covered with new fabric a few times to keep them looking new and stylish. Many people during those days had their furniture

---

[129] Psalm 139:23-24 (NLT).

upholstered or re-covered because it was less expensive than buying new furniture. The idea was to make the old look new again.

Sometimes with that furniture, we thought it would only need a new outer covering. Once the upholsterer examined it thoroughly, he might find that the stuffing inside also needed to be replaced. Sometimes parts of the wood frame had to be replaced. Much could be hidden below the outer layer!

Isn't this what Jesus does for us? When we surrender to Him, He looks deep inside to find all that is not like Him. Then He covers us with His blood and makes us a new creation. He continues to cleanse us so that we can become more like Him.

This is more than simply a new covering or a change of the outside appearance. We become new from the inside out. Thank you, Jesus!

We Are In Transformation = WAIT!

> "Wait on the LORD; Be of good courage,
> And He shall strengthen your heart;
> Wait, I say, on the LORD!"[130]

In a previous message, God was telling me to wait on Him rather than try to handle projects myself. And now, He just gave me a sequel to that message!

He is telling me to *WAIT* right now. I don't know for how long or why, but I know what He put into my spirit so I will wait on Him. He has a very consistent track record with me! How about you? Are you in a waiting season too? Maybe we need to remember Psalm 27:14!

As I was driving to Chase City this morning, my mind was still focused on *WAIT*, and I wondered if that word was an acronym from God. I began to insert words for each letter, and after about 5 minutes, this is what God gave me:

W - We
A - Are
I - In
T - Transformation

When God is asking us to **WAIT** on Him, He is saying that **W**e **A**re **I**n **T**ransformation. He has everything under control, but He is

---
[130] Psalm 27:14 (NKJV).

changing us while He is working on our circumstances. But God, why? Can't you just handle things and leave us the way we are? What does waiting do for us personally??

When transformation takes place during our waiting, it means there is movement or development from one form or type to another. God is moving us or developing us from where/what we were before to where/what He wants us to be.

Thinking about the words "courage" and "strength" in the scripture above, I found their definitions:

"Be of good courage":

- Dictionary.com – "the quality of mind or spirit that enables a person to face difficulty, danger, pain, etc., without fear; bravery"[131]
- Strong's Concordance – to fasten upon; be strong[132]

God is telling us to stay close to Him; fasten ourselves to Him; be strong; keep our mind and spirit strong to face what's ahead with bravery.

"And He shall strengthen your heart":

- Cambridge Dictionary – to make something stronger or more effective[133]
- Strong's Concordance – to be alert; be courageous; steadfastly minded, strong, establish, fortify[134]

---

[131] *Dictionary*, Random House Unabridged Dictionary, "Courage", https://www.dictionary.com/browse/courage.

[132] James Strong, *Strong's Expanded Exhaustive Concordance of the Bible*, (Tennessee, Thomas Nelson, 2001), 83.

[133] *Dictionary*, Cambridge Advanced Learner's Dictionary & Thesaurus, "Strengthen", https://dictionary.cambridge.org/us/dictionary/english/strengthen.

[134] James Strong, *Strong's Expanded Exhaustive Concordance of the Bible*, (Tennessee, Thomas Nelson, 2001), 22.

God is saying that He is making us stronger and more effective to do what He has assigned us to do. He has us in transformation in order to make us more alert, to establish us where He wants us, and to fortify us in our physical and mental strength.

We all know that God is working on our behalf *ALL THE TIME*! This scripture helps us to understand what He is doing for us. Not that we really need to know, but it does help me to have some idea of why I have to wait. It is not always about what God is handling for each of our situations, but it is also about what He is doing in and through us. I do believe it is worth the wait!

What Happens to All of the Fallen Leaves?

> "He shall be like a tree
> Planted by the rivers of water,
> That brings forth its fruit in its season,
> Whose leaf also shall not wither;
> And whatever he does shall prosper."[135]

While exercising on our elliptical machine this morning, I saw lots of leaves from our silver maple laying on the ground. There are still many leaves left on the tree so the ground will be covered in the next few days/weeks. I wondered why God led my eyes to these leaves. What does this mean to the body of Christ? Do they represent members of the body who have fallen from Christ? Do they represent members of the body whom God has sent to the ground (or into the world) to fertilize that ground with God's Word and Truth? These leaves will never return to that tree as a leaf. What does this mean, God?

> "Since leaves have water inside their cells, they can't survive freezing temperatures, because the water would freeze and the leaves would die. When leaves fall to the ground, they eventually break down and provide nutrients for the soil, helping prepare for

---

[135] Psalm 1:3 (NKJV).

more plants to grow in the spring and also create a layer that helps the ground absorb water." [136]

Every fallen leaf is still living and will take on a new form to provide what the soil needs. This helps to prepare more plants to grow in the spring. Do you see? God is telling us that each leaf (us as members of the body) continues to have purpose as we relocate to a different environment/different season in our lives and in another form. We become a "new creation"[137]

A farmer plows the ground so that air and elements can be absorbed into it, which will bring about a bountiful crop. Our purpose is to help break down the soil (minds of others) so that God's Holy Spirit can seep into it along with His Word. He asks us to teach or spread His Word to others wherever we are. In the spring of our season, we will thank God for His fertilization that has taken place as we see not only more trees/plants emerging and growing into mature plants but also more faith-filled believers in Christ. It is all a God-process but one which brings new life – to our planet and to our spirits!

At this time of Thanks and Giving to others, let us all remember that God deserves our thanks and giving every day of every year, regardless of what we are facing and going through. Why? Because it all came from Him in the first place. Blessings to you all!

---

[136] "What Are Leaves For?", https://learning-center.homesciencetools.com/article/learn-about-leaves/, 2021 Home Science Tools.
[137] 2 Corinthians 5:17 (NKJV).

Who's Behind that Curtain?

"The curtain of the temple was torn in two from top to bottom."[138]

When I was growing up, I could not watch "The Wizard of Oz" after seeing it the first time. Those monkeys and the Wicked Witch of the West scared me so badly! Was anyone else afraid of them?? Whenever the movie came on, my brother was right in front of the TV, and I was in another room trying not to hear any sound from the movie!

Nevertheless, do you remember the part when Dorothy and the gang were talking to the Great Wizard behind the curtain, and Toto trotted over to pull the curtain back? The Wizard was not a real wizard after all but a "humbug circus performer"[139]. However, he was not revealed nor made accessible until Toto pulled that curtain back. When Dorothy accosted him for trying to be something he was not, he simply said "No dear, I'm a very good man. Just a very bad wizard."

Dorothy and the gang thought that they were at the mercy of this "wizard" regarding Dorothy's return to Kansas and that his "super" power would help her return. What disappointment for them when they saw that the wizard was a regular man. He had no more "super" power than they did.

---

[138] Mark 15:38 (NIV)
[139] Fleming, Victor, dir. *The Wizard of Oz*, 1939, Metro-Goldwyn-Mayer, 1 hour 52 minutes, https://en.wikipedia.org/wiki/List_of_Oz_characters_(created_by_Baum)#Wizard_of_Oz.

During this morning's quiet time, I was thanking and praising God for giving us his only Son to die on the cross and tear down that veil in order for us to have open access to Him. He instantly gave me the vision of the Wizard behind the curtain. But why? Why did God give me this vision?

Before the plan of redemption, God was "located" in the holiest of holies behind a veil in the tabernacle, and only the high priest could have access to him. Once a year, the priest would take a blood sacrifice to God to plead the sins of the people. He wore bells around the bottom of his robe. If the people outside didn't hear the bells, they would assume that the priest had died in the sight of God and would pull him out.

But God wanted to be with his people more directly. He had a plan of redemption! When Jesus died and the veil was torn from top to bottom, God moved out of that place in the tabernacle never to dwell again in a temple made by hands. Everyone, even the Gentiles, had full and direct access to God. The process changed from praying to God through clergy or some other intercessor to having a direct, personal relationship with God!

In the Wizard of Oz, the "Wizard" wanted to have power and be important so the people would "worship" him and seek his advice. But the only way he could claim this power was to hide behind a curtain.

In God's case, the situation was opposite. He already had the ultimate power but was located in the holiest of holies. He wanted to be with his people. When Jesus made the ultimate sacrifice and tore down that veil, God was made accessible to all of us for a personal, direct relationship. We don't have to talk through someone else to God. We talk directly to Him! How awesome is that?

Unlike the "humbug circus performer", our God is one who didn't want to remain hidden. He loves His people with an awesome, unconditional love and now is always with us and in us. He put the right plan into action so that we didn't have to ask, "Who's Behind that Curtain"!

Who Are You Standing Next To?

"Let us hold fast the confession of our hope without wavering, for He who promised is faithful. And let us consider one another in order to stir up love and good works, not forsaking the assembling of ourselves together, as is the manner of some, but exhorting one another, and so much the more as you see the Day approaching."[140]

"Since God's enemies will fall, don't stand next to them."[141]

It's the kind of quote that stops you for a second or two, and then you think, "Well, of course, God's enemies will fall! God wins every time!" You know it is true but don't always hear it stated in a way such as this.

This led me to think about who I spend my time with; who I associate with; who I seek counsel from; who I try to serve and minister to. Am I surrounding myself with the people He wants me to? Who am I standing next to?

All of us need to have a group as well as individual friends who are saved through Christ and part of the Kingdom of God. I have two recent experiences which God used to emphasize this to me:

A Bible Study group, which I have attended for a few months, recently had a luncheon. This is a group of godly women who want

---

[140] Hebrews 10:23-25 (NKJV).
[141] Teacher's Guide, "Partners in a New Creation" series (Isaiah, John, Revelation); Standardlesson.com, Summer 2022, June, July, August, NIV.

nothing more than to continue to learn the Word of God and how to live it and share it better. There were several comments about what this group has meant to each woman. Several expressed difficult times they had been through, but the steadfastness and love of this group helped them along the way. It was good to be surrounded by these Godly women!

On another day, there were 4 of us sharing lunch together. It had been months since we were last together in person. After sharing, laughing, and even shedding some tears, we closed our time in prayer. My heart was so full... full of gratitude to God for bringing us together; full of love for each sister and her walk with God; full of faith in the God who is constant. It was good to be surrounded by these Godly women! God's enemies will surely fall, but we mustn't fall with them. We must ALL make sure we are surrounded by people God directs us to.

"And let us consider one another in order to *stir up* love and good works, not forsaking the *assembling of ourselves together*, as is the manner of some, but *exhorting* one another, and so much the more as you see the Day approaching." (emphasis mine)

In verse 25 of the Hebrews scripture, there are several points to restate from the NKJV Study Bible notes:

- *stir up* – speaks forcefully of the tremendous impact that believers can have on each other.
- *assembling of ourselves together* – evidently some believers had stopped attending the worship service of the church perhaps because they feared persecution
- *exhorting* – coming alongside and inspiring another with the truth. The local assembly is where the gospel message is preached, but also where the word of God is applied to the circumstances of our lives.[142]

---

[142] New King James Version Study Bible, Tennessee, Thomas Nelson, 1982, page 1873.

❖ Rachel Jolly West ❖

Many have left the church over the past 2-3 years due to COVID and other personal reasons. What has this gained them? What have they lost? I believe this scripture answers those questions about the fellowship with believers, the encouragement of believers, the "stirred up" love and good works of believers – all with the ultimate goal of serving and praising God and *being the presence of God* to others. As individuals, we are mighty in God as we carry out the plans He has for us. As the body of Christ, we can do ALL things through Christ Jesus!

Who are you standing next to? Have you surrounded yourself with Godly people and those God directs you to? Is this where God wants you to be? Let us all continue in unity to bring others into the body of Christ so that we may ALL stand for Christ and build His Kingdom!

About The Author

In November 2020, Rachel felt God's nudging to compile her blog messages into her first book, *The View From My Window: A Walk With God* for people around the world. In July 2022, she felt Him nudging her again to publish a second book by giving her the book title and the cover picture. This book will take you "Beyond the Window: Inside your Heart".

Rachel grew up in Clarksville VA, the only lake town located on Buggs Island Lake. She served as a recreational therapy director in a hospital and in a developmental center for individuals with intellectual disabilities. After retirement, she returned to Clarksville with her husband. Here is where the new adventure began!

Rachel lives with her husband, Pastor Mike West, and loves gardening flowers and vegetables, hiking, kayaking, or anything outside! They have two grown sons who live with their families in NC and DE. Rachel and Mike have several grandchildren whom they adore.

If you would like to communicate with Rachel, you may contact her through her website www.rachelwestauthor.com where you will find dates/locations of her book signings, or her book's FaceBook page, https://www.facebook.com/rachelwestauthor. You may find both of Rachel's books at Amazon.com and BarnesandNoble.com. You may also enjoy her blog at www.simplify10.com. Feel free to share feedback about the book as well as your spiritual journey.